ETHNOGRAPHY #9

ETHNOGRAPHY #9

ALAN KLIMA

DUKE UNIVERSITY PRESS   DURHAM AND LONDON   2019

© 2019 DUKE UNIVERSITY PRESS
All rights reserved
Printed in the United States of America
on acid-free paper ∞
Designed by Matthew Tauch
Typeset in Merope and Cronos Pro
by Copperline Book Services

The Cataloging-in-Publication Data is available
at the Library of Congress.
ISBN 978-1-4780-0711-1 (ebook)
ISBN 978-1-4780-0544-5 (hardcover)
ISBN 978-1-4780-0621-3 (paperback)

This title is freely available in an open access
edition thanks to the TOME initiative and the
generous support of the University of California,
Davis. Learn more at openmonographs.org.

Cover art by Matthew Tauch, based on photographs
by Alan Klima

CONTENTS

ACKNOWLEDGMENTS

I OWE A TREMENDOUS DEBT, which will never be repaid, to Bank of America. (Note that parts of this acknowledgment, not to mention the text that follows it, may be false, and no acknowledgement of actual debt — or intention of repayment — is intended or implied.) Of course, as will become eminently clear in what is to follow, the greatest debt of all is to my, as it were, "visitor," with whom I have struggled for so long. Rather than cover that debt up by using seamless continuities to selectively write her into the text, or writing her out for that matter, I leave within the text the traces of our exchanges and negotiations, the abrupt disjunctures in our conflicting purposes, to remain as material evidence of this debt to her and to our struggle.

I also greatly appreciate the feedback from Joe Dumit, Marisol de la Cadena, Chris Kortright, Jacob Culbertson, Adrian Yen, Cristiana Giordano, Tarek Elhaik, anonymous reviewers, and Gisela Fosado, and I especially acknowledge their recognition that there is value in sometimes contemplating the kind of thought that cannot be directly stated, but that can be said.

1 · THE GHOST MANIFESTO

THERE ARE HUMANS STALKING THE WORLD OF SPECTERS. They want something from these spirits, and they return again and again to them, seemingly relentless. This is obvious everywhere you look, especially in narrative film in the global market but also in all the ruminations over digital transformation in the world over an ethereal realm of numbers and representation, which seems to almost beckon for metaphors of ghosts and spirits. That humans are stalking the spirit world is apparent everywhere you look, although I myself, at least in my capacity as a finite mortal, cannot look everywhere.

And yet there is a certain value to embracing that fact, and instead turning to look nowhere, no place. This series of meditations on the past in Thailand, *Ethnography #9*, is the ninth in a series of meditations on no place, the previous editions of which may or may not have ever existed.

There are humans stalking the spirit world. This is not restful, nor a sign of rest, nor something that can rest or be put to rest. The digital instantiation of social realities proliferates with such obvious relentlessness, and there are groping critical hands reaching for the spirit world, and this will not stop or lie still. And what is owed in return?

How do you understand this spirit world? Is the spirit world fiction? Is it true but unknowable? Is the spirit world a product of primitive fetishism or simply inappropriate subject matter for enlightened social science to engage with, or is there some other way in which it is to be separated, barred?

And what are you, then, in relation to it?

Dubbing the Numberstream

You would not know at first glance that the room is actually built of old teak boards, because the old wood is shellacked to a point approaching vinyl. The house is built to last. For insurance, there are photos of family ancestors, kings, and Buddhist saints hung all along one wall as well as bright-red protective flags hung near every door on which arcane inscriptions of numbers and sacred alphabets are inked into complex matrices designed to cheat fate.

The brand-new flat-screen here in this Northern Thai house plays over and over the images from exactly halfway around the world of two planes crashing into New York City, of explosions, of two tall white buildings tumbling down and lashing out with giant paws of dust.

Kamnoi, in her sixties with failing eyes, is latched to the set. With her notebook and pen in hand, she searches the screen through big frog-goggle glasses. Her jet-black wig is tilted off-kilter, but she takes no notice. A plane hits; she writes down the time. A building crashes; that gets jotted down too. The colors of the smoke, the shape of the rubble, and the numbers estimated to have died, all these are inscribed as quickly as Kamnoi can perceive them or can receive information from the on-the-fly Thai translations of live video feed that chime in and out of the foreign broadcast almost randomly.

Interpretation runs in her family. As a young woman she would attend the backyard cinema her neighbor would set up on Sundays, where it was her uncle who served as the voiceover translator and dubber for Hollywood films, although he knew no English. Sitting in the back, throwing his voice through a PA system, he would ventriloquize whatever he decided the characters might be saying to each other. A deep voice for men, a high voice for women. The drama did not suffer, Kamnoi has insisted on several occasions.

Her notebook is a mess of observations, readings, and numbers. "These are the raw events," she explains. "The rawness is the misfortune. But it leaves a hole in the world. And to that hole of extraordinary misfortune, fortune is drawn. Then you have to pull out the cooked meaning, and you get the number."

As Kamnoi moves quickly but calmly, my own mind is spinning political nightmare stories and future scenarios (which, it so happened, paled in comparison to reality). I am comforted by Kamnoi's combination of assurance in the future and her whatever-will-be-will-be attitude. If she gets the right numbers, she will know soon enough.

But in a few days it will become apparent that they are not the right numbers. Actually, she could have won if she had not spent today decoding her TV set and had instead gone out to the market, where she normally would have gone had none of this happened exactly halfway around the world. If she were in the market, she would be privy to the general consensus, which is short and sweet not to mention correct. There are four planes, and two buildings have gone down. Four and two are the hot numbers. Everyone in the local market is going to clean up.

Meanwhile, the bet takers in the local underground lottery (which uses the last numbers of the government lottery number drawing) will lose big and almost be bankrupted, as sometimes happens when a large social body cooks the raw event in just the right way.

Kamnoi is one of innumerable people in her rural Northern Thai district who spend a considerable portion of their lives attending to the world for the numerical communications lying behind its appearances. And it is 2001 by Christian accounting, which is not quite foreign to her or anyone around here, where it is also 2544 in the Buddhist calendar. It does seem like the first year of a new millennium. But we are not going forward much here. This is, more or less, the end. That millennium will not ever come, as we know. But here, now, near the end of time for Kamnoi, opportunities for numerical perception come while she is reeling from the financial catastrophe of the Asian financial crisis that has just unfolded over recent years. This happens to be a place severely impacted by the spread of neoliberal discourses of financial liberalization, which set up conditions of capital free-flow and financial panic and set in motion a painful aftermath of unemployment, inflation, and economic stagnation that is still very much present now, materially, as the trade towers come crashing down. And that was that. War, destruction, hate, loudness, the end of the human race, and the destruction of the planet followed, and we all know how that turned out, so we will not go further into all that came after life was over.

Instead it is here, in this conjuncture between two different lives of numbers, and on this exact position in the line of past time, that I wish to drop the question of fantasy and the real. On one side lies financial liberalization, with its global imagination about a most abstract sense of monetary value that was to be set free to live as pure number in a deterritorialized and digitally mediated virtual environment in which it could roam and trade freely without limit. On the other side are those impacted by this regime of numbers but who are, in their turn, at least as ardently engaged in an abstract realm of numbers and fortune, all the more so as the money has dried up in all other economic forms beyond the quick wins and losses of gambling on numbers. And there may be, of course, no coincidental relation just at this moment between these two numerical worlds.

But, then again, this is also fiction, because there never was such a thing as "this moment," any more than there is a "this moment" now that it is all over. You can check this for yourself. Just look for the present, and what you will see is a memory of the near past drifting ever away, crumbling, unsteady. There is only the past, and not even that can be grasped.

Still, one might be tempted to cling to something other than time, at least, as real. One might be tempted to designate these animated realms of numbers — if we understand Marx's idea that they are, ultimately, themselves also bizarre social containers of labor "time" — as somehow unreal, yet with reality effects. What, then, to do with the fact that digital markets of currency exchange, derivatives, and abstract monetary entities and futures are traded in nominal volumes that dwarf in thousandfolds the commodity economy and occasionally crash with extreme fury to suddenly scorch people, creatures, land and air and water? Some abstraction, right? This conjures up something that seems almost an autonomous power: the notion that abstract time-value exchange realms could be apart in their nature let alone trickle out from themselves with value.

By contrast, the world of divination, ghosts, and specters is famously regarded — in certain circles around and about the world — as being wholly dependent on cultural constitution and only possibly, just possibly, touching the real occasionally (while many would completely disagree).

But there is, in my estimation, a profound irony involved in a realist discipline like anthropology as it peers into the realm of fantasy (and this is a problem of interpretation compounded by the long-standing association of capital with fantasy in critical theory). The problem that insists and intrudes here is how an anthropology of fantasy might tend to cast both the documentarian of fantasy and the inspected content of fantasy itself "in the land of the real." In other words, one presumes that any dream content that appears before the documentarian's view is really there, that is, that the documentarian of fantasy is working with and through "really existing fantasies" and is not making them up, hallucinating, or even substantially duped by their own inherent or constructed desires.

Not to mention the belief that we already know that the documentarian, the author, or the writer is her- or himself real, and we already know very well just what sort of a thing that being is.

No more thought or attention to this matter need detain us. One may write about fantasy, but what one writes is, on balance, not fantasy but reality delivered in a realist frame.[1]

And one knows who or what one is.

This realist frame becomes doubly privileged when we bring fantasy and capital together, no doubt beginning at least with Marx, or so it seems to me, and the fanciful images of commodity fetishism that he drew of men chasing, interacting with, speaking to, and finally bowing down before animated fantasies of value without seeing that they were, in fact, their own creations. Of course, in this playful image that Marx causes to arise, there is a certain sense in which the ardent capitalists imagine nothing but, in fact, accurately perceive the real state of value under a social regime of commodity fetishism. But what they lack, as Marx makes evident through his tropes, is a conscious sense of the fantastic to it all, of all the human creation and the ordering of this codification of desire. Or that is how I would prefer to phrase it. One could also draw on the colonialist frame of "fetishism," the thought-world of the "primitive," for a trope (or rather, is it not meant almost literally?) that can capture the lack of enlightened perception into things as they really are.

The extrapolation of Marx's read on abstract monetary value into other cultural realms of fantasy has, of course, been much elaborated over the previous century, especially enabled by Freud's tactics of dream reading back to primary messages displaced in dreamwork and all the analogies it became possible to draw with primary social conflicts and their expression in the cultural life of groups. Arguably, though, the analysis of dream and capital has returned full circle as it contemplates forms of life tendered in abstract monetary entities; the digitized and globalized realm of financial communication; and the space, time, territory, and sovereignty it re-forms and deforms. Figures of the spirit world, the spectral and ethereal, seem to beg to be used to describe this, and, of course, they have been used, particularly within critical logics of debt and haunting.

There the spectral functions as metaphor and trope. Famously with Slavoj Žižek revenants return from death as the "collectors of some unpaid symbolic debt" and represent "the fundamental fantasy of contemporary mass culture."[2] The ethereal is the sovereign metaphor for global empire in the work of Michael Hardt and Antonio Negri.[3] Cultural geography has a "spectral turn" that Emilie Cameron has so pointedly exposed for its exploitation of spectral imagery that reproduces colonial power relations.[4] This tapping into the spirit world in social theory, of course, begins at least as far back as Marx.

And what if there were a different question than that critically posed most often to the liberal use of spectral metaphors in thought about the expanding virtual world? The common reaction to the overuse of spiritualist metaphors to contemplate the digital future is to demand that we be shown the insides of the black box: the material realities, the precise wirings and apparatuses, their global routes covered and passed over, and the social structure that enables their construction in a way that grounds analyses of the virtual world in actual material relations, networks, or hardware. In fact, such questions are not inherently inimical to spectral theory of globalization, as, after all, a notion of an actual physical material world was, in fact, where Marx seemed to be headed when he first invoked the images of so-called primitive fetishism and exposed capitalists as new pagans with occluded vision.

Of course, there was even then, no less than today, nothing entirely new about the propagation of haunting and scary stories of economic change, of the bodily and material transmogrification of value into the fantastical immaterial recomposed into increasingly abstract realms. It is one of the most common plot movements in the genre of economic horror stories. Even Adam Smith propagated this fear in his story of money and its evolution out of barter and trade into equivalency devices of valuable objects such as gold.[5] However, that is all backstory; the real story begins to move at the point where one had to be sure that the gold in the coin was pure and was actually the weight claimed. And in order to make this certain, the sovereign would place his stamp and face upon the gold to certify its proper value. Eventually, however, what happened was that the stamp began to become more important than the gold, and the face on the gold became, with paper currency, value in itself, representing a deposit of gold held elsewhere. Adam Smith feared the day when value would become all stamp . . . the face of the sovereign divorced from its material embodiment like a ghostly visage and trace, seen but not bodily present in the full. At that point of rupture with the body . . .

an invitation to the wildest speculations . . .

breaks with gravity . . .

without limits, material constraints, while we here, down on earth, are compelled to live, still in our bodies, and the value we have created is granted a freedom we can never have . . .

and then even the ghostly face disappears and only the number remains, virtually without form . . .

and, therefore, a freed human imagination could have the power of return, to insert itself into the very fabric of the most utilitarian aspects of human exchange and stake its claim . . .

Insistent and Real

These stories of the Nextworld from the 2500s (the Buddhist era) of ghosts and numbers, from the times of pre- and postcrashing Thailand, are stories about something missing, about debt and haunting, about the insistence of a strange hollowness, palpable yet invisible for the most part. This non-thing that debt and haunting share.

What I mean by that which is missing yet present is not like the status of reality in fiction, the missing bit of reality-ness in an otherwise convincing fictional world, that shadowland of narrative where we suspend our disbelief and therefore experience the strange light of an unreal real. I do not mean to call attention to similar "fictions" of money and spirits. It is easy enough to imagine that money has no value apart from that fictionally ascribed to it in a system of convention, commodities, or so-called fetishism. And it would be easy enough to stress that, at bottom, money, like ghosts, is empty.

Of course, when such things are said of money in social science, it is meant only to heighten our sense of the social reality, that socially, money is very real, and therefore, in its social space, it impacts people with all the effects of a socially enforced *but therefore also socially changeable* reality.

This absence of substance, with all the effects of being substantial, might be comparable to or even serve as the mirror image of the spirit world, at least from a certain anthropological perspective. There, too, it is said, the fictions of spiritual entities are formed in systems of conventions, shared beliefs, language, and media. For those who believe or inhabit the "worldview," there are very real consequences of the agreed fictions of spirits in social space not to mention in the vibrations of intimate affect. And this only serves to heighten the reality effect that an anthropological author can transmit.

But all that social construction, you see, is only one side of the story. The whole world can seem to be understood with only that side of the story. Money, persons, the whole world can fit this picture of social construction, with all its people and animals, its forests and seas, its global connections and disjunctures, its dreamworlds and beliefs, its wired and wireless networks of information and values circulating over the surface of the earth. I, too, see that world.

But I can also see another.

A Haunted Teak Pillar

We all call him Uncle Wua, an old man who listens in on our conversations under the shade of the stilted house, talk that always makes its way around to the subject of money. As he is paralyzed, he is laid out there every day on his bamboo platform to while away the daytime hours. He is always there, hovering half a meter in the air, an almost-but-not-quite-unnoticed reminder of the call that ghosts and spirits of the dead have on the wealth of this world.

Old Uncle Wua had been in good health and spirits back in the 1980s, when this stilted house was built and the local economy was in the prime of adolescence and had started to spurt, especially invigorated by those plugged into the power plant run by the Thai state and staffed by members of the most powerful union in the kingdom, the Union of Electricity

Workers. That was the time when all the building and construction took off. Years of salaried work had slowly built up in the local economy to what seemed like a sudden tipping point in the late eighties, when everyone who could manage would become singularly focused on building the best house that money could buy.

And nothing was better in the category of best, nothing so signaled the embodiment of wealth, than wood. Teak, that is. Endangered. Regulated and therefore usually illegal. Precious beyond compare. You put in an order with the right person (and everyone knows who that is), and the teak is delivered to the construction site in the middle of the night. No one ever died at the point of delivery. It was only people out chopping it down in the forest or people carting it off in pickups or the occasional police officer who failed to obey the chain of command, pay-off, and territorial boundary who was offed in some offhand way, usually by a bullet in the head and two in the chest, somewhere off in the distance where an ordinary consumer's thoughts rarely roamed.

It is not only the endangered rarity of teak that makes of it such a solid embodiment of the idea of wealth. It is also that it is, quite plainly, hard. Solid hardwood that comes from massive, tall trees. Nowadays, as the government has relaxed restrictions on cutting down trees on your own property in order to encourage the home cultivation of teak, fields everywhere in Northern Thailand have become populated with teak trunks arrayed in something like a military review. You can see almost endlessly into the depths of the tree grids since the low-lying leaves and branches are shorn off to encourage faster growth of the trunk, straight up in the air, and for packing in tighter rows and columns. Before the new government policy, there was no incentive to plot these graphs of trees since the ordinary person would not risk cutting down teak on his own property, as it would be obvious who did it, while only the Thai Forestry Department had the legal right to fell a teak tree.

Of course, teak's value also derives from its long use and association with the home, as it makes a great board, hard yet flexible under foot and weight while also having little expansion or contraction with fluctuations of humidity compared to many other species. But in matters of building impressive homes, it is not the usefulness of boards that signals the solidity of value so much as it is the trunk itself. Fronting the home with at least two columns, like two hard slaps in the face, the solid trunk of teak is the only absolutely essential element of an inspiring house. Such pillars of teak trunk contain the as-yet-unformed potential of the tree and yet are harvested, in possession, the stored potential of teak wood ready at any moment to become teak boards, furniture, ornament. It is, in a sense, a formless, fungible sort of wealth in that it carries the potential to become many things. For those who can manage, every stilt of the house should be a big, dense, solid teak trunk, the fatter the better. In the best case, all the boards of the house should also be teak. Cement should appear only sparingly, in the bathroom or kitchen perhaps, or perhaps the rear stilts, or nowhere at all. But most important are the two frontal pillars of solid, sanded and stained but otherwise uncut trunks of tree.

Few obtain the ideal for the whole house, and Uncle Wua was no exception, and this is what renders the two frontal pillars all the more important, as everyone can be sure to be compared there at least. It is there where you put in your best effort to bring to material fruition the solidity of your position in the realm of wealth. And as the disciplined rows of new teak-tree fields have begun to report to duty, it is even more true than ever to say that, in a sense, one builds one's house literally out of wealth. Not just with wealth, but with wealth itself as a building material and the most important one at that.

Uncle Wua, back in the days when he was in good health, had managed to get two massive teak trunks delivered in the middle of the night. He was, it turned out, the happiest he ever again would be when he woke up that morning. They were not tall trunks, as they would only be frontal pillars to support a small veranda. But they were thick and heavy enough. Really heavy.

He was, and still is, a nice man, a good man. A guy like that marries quickly and easily. The mother of the bride likes him as much as her daughter does and tends to be content with less bride price, or "mother's milk" compensation, than she might be were he different. So things like that go smoothly. But often they do not stay that way because, as with all good men, there was no avoiding the fact that other ladies would perceive this good heart as well. And it was not such a bad thing in his mind or in the minds of most men he knew to occasionally fool around with women. Or, as it were, many women, or, as it were, rather often, or perhaps the best way to put it would be practically all the time. His wife would alternate between knowing it, not wanting to know it, "not knowing it," getting into jealous rages, and gambling here and there in her spare time in quiet desperation and treasuring her favorite possessions, most of all a big, thick gold chain, her favorite piece of jewelry of which she was quite proud.

Things went on like this for her until she died of cancer, as many do in the area. Soon after, Uncle Wua fell in love. Too soon, it turned out. But he was sincere enough. He may have even been faithful to her (although he is not so forthcoming with the personal details the closer the story gets in time to the incident).

But even after a few years, his wife did not fade from the picture. One night, a friend came to stay in Uncle Wua's house for a couple of weeks, and his wife came as well. Uncle Wua put them up in what had been his wife's room. The very first night, as soon as they put the lights out, they heard creaking footsteps in and around their room but thought nothing of it as it was probably Wua. But why it sounded like he was in their room, they could not say. The next night, they went out drinking and on to the village temple where there was a fair where you could pay to dance with young women for five *baht* a dance. Uncle Wua, especially, had a blast dancing the night away with the women.

But when they all got home, they found, to their great alarm, that all the lights, which they had left off, were on brightly in every room. They were all afraid of robbers, but as they crept up silently to the door and slipped in, they found no one there. Instead, they found spoons from the kitchen scattered on the living room floor.

That night, when the couple went to sleep, the husband swore he woke up, or half woke up, in the middle of the night and saw red eyes peering at him through the window. The red eyes made him feel faint, and he collapsed back to sleep.

The next day they convinced themselves that it had been a cat, somehow hanging from a branch, or a dream.

During the next night, the couple woke up together, and with a sudden shock, they saw looming up over them and right next to the bed the angry red eyes and the form of a pale woman. At first they could not move away from the thing at the bedside, the side of the bed that had once been that of the dead wife. But eventually they regained the use of their muscles and sprang forth and ran out of the room and out of the house. They had to be coaxed back in but refused, in any case, to sleep in that room again.

Around that time, Uncle Wua's new girlfriend came to him, asking him permission to sell the gold chain he had given her. In fact, it had been his former wife's favorite chain, and he had had bad dreams from the moment he had first given it to his girlfriend. Now she wanted to sell his wife's gold chain to help with the debt payments she was in for with a local money-lender, which she had contracted in building her own new house. As Uncle Wua was in the midst of building his, he could hardly fail to sympathize and quickly agreed to the idea.

His wife, apparently, felt differently. The dreams became worse. At the end he could not sleep. He would lie on his back and stare at the ceiling. Every night, after an hour or so, he would become aware of a figure standing beside him. He could not turn his eyes toward it, so he would close them for a while, hoping it would go away. But when he opened them, it would still be there. He definitely was not sleeping or dreaming, he says, because he was too scared to sleep. He would open his eyes again, and the thing would still be there, and he would see it from the corner of his eyes, staring at him. Then, as the night wore on, it would try to touch his face, and he would go into a frozen-still frenzy. Finally he would become weak and faint, fall asleep, and then wake again in early dawn with a twitch of his whole body and a gasp of cold, wet morning air.

One day, soon after the sale of her gold chain, while Uncle Wua was looking around his construction site and talking to the builder, one of his big teak pillars fell down, hard, on top of him. The dense, heavy tree trunk pinned him down at the small of the back, and he was screaming and pounding the ground with his palms.

They eventually rolled the teak trunk up off him, though he himself never did get up ever again, at least not without being pulled up by others. The bad dreams and visitations stopped after that, but the punishment has worn on to this day, every day, as poor uncle Wua lies paralyzed on his bamboo platform while the really living live out their lives around him.

An injustice, perhaps, in some worldly calculus of economical punishment. But the ghost of his wife was operating with otherworldly anger about her gold. It is dangerous and unpredictable to ignore the hold that is placed on valuable things. As the seemingly material embodiment of value, such things already seem in their nature embedded in two places at once, as idea and as matter. If matter is something that is even possible. For if the universe is actually made of this so-called matter, and if ideas

□ material world the mere notion

are simply notions inexactly correlated to this material universe, then this reach of the idea to topple upon a man is impossible.

Yet, if it happens, could it be that it is the material world that is the mere notion?

At least we can say that when a ghost lashes out, available to it are other things that seem to be in two places at once, things of value, no matter how seemingly solid, no matter how apparently dense. In this case it is precisely the density of teak that embodies the traversing hold of wealth.

But that is not the only sense in which the ideas of matter and bodies of this world are seized by a beyond, by autonomously consensual value, or by the possible impossibility of this divide being real.

The Suicide Tree

It is impossible to walk past a "luscious tree," a *don cham chaa*, without wondering whether anyone has ever hanged himself there. Or if someone will one day.

"Cham chaa" is expressive of juicy, vibrant green life, a long-living tree with exposed roots like a shaggy dog paw, thick branches and leaves. A perfect shade tree for the increasingly barren and hot countryside of Northern Thailand. But not a soul would seek a cham chaa tree for relief. You walk past just as fast as you can, try not to look, try not to wonder.

Once, in the 1970s, there used to be a cham chaa tree that everyone had to walk past when entering or leaving Jai Village. It was not far behind the ornate red gate of the village that fronts what is now a busy road to the power station. It grew tall in the cremation area that flanks the village temple, which was what made the tree even more creepy.

This is the area where the dead are burned. Corpses are placed on a pile of wood but also mixed with old tires so that the oily burn is hot enough to melt sinews and cartilage, which do not give up easily. Sometimes the heat is too little, such that it merely pulls on the body's strings, and the corpse sits up suddenly in the fire, raising its arms stiffly and hissing a crazed shower of black ash.

When the corpse sits up, naturally many people scream and some run all the way home. But, of course, a sudden reanimation on the pyre is not itself real haunting. Lek, the funeral groundsperson of Jai Village, says that to him, it is old fare. There is nothing especially scary about a cremation grounds for him, and the sight of corpses burning could never become associated in his mind with the sight of a great cham chaa tree hovering over the dispatches of the dead. But the emotions were different for the others. He had been in the grounds a long while, and he was even there watching with his father, who was also a funeral groundsperson, when the entire village marched into the charnel ground to chop down that luscious tree and then madly hack up its stump and burn its roots until there was no trace.

They do not always do that to a cham chaa tree, which is why you have to wonder when you walk past one. Maybe someone hanged himself there, maybe not. It is dark under the tree, even in the day. Its scraggly branches are strong, hang low to the ground, are easily climbed and inviting. That may be part of the reason people always seem to choose it in which to kill themselves.

Chopping down a haunted tree is usually a last resort. The first recourse is a powerful ritual to "suck" the spirit out of the tree. The tree is wrapped round and round with blessing string, a simple white twine, and the blessing string is held in the palms of nine Buddhist monks who stand, encircling the trunk, chanting for hours around the suicide tree until they have the spirit drawn out of the wood and back into the proper, intermediary realm for the recently dead, neither completely passed nor completely here. But something had happened with that cham chaa tree of Jai Village that roiled things to another level.

Back then, Mr. Gongkam had been a truck driver. Perhaps more often than anyone else, he drove past that cham chaa tree in front of Jai Village. Gongkam had his own truck in a time, the early 1970s, when few had more than a bicycle. He would hire himself and his truck out for the long hauls over the mountain passes to the northern border towns and outposts of the kingdom. It was rough riding before they started carving big paved highways into the mountains as an anticommunist strategic policy, years later.

Actually, the story of the tree all started round about then, in the 1970s, when his life on the road seemed like it was about to get a whole lot smoother. But his truck broke down to an extent beyond his economic means to repair. Gongkam was already in trouble with debts, and people were angry with him about that. He did have a sister, who had become relatively wealthy as the main groceries dealer in Jai, who was, however, notorious for her stinginess even, or even especially, among relatives. Gongkam beseeched his elder sister to borrow the money to fix his truck. After all, he had a family riding on this. For several days he talked and talked about his troubles with everyone, getting more and more visibly unhinged. How could his own blood do this to him? His own sister was sucking the life from him, for without the cash, the whole scheme would crash: no truck, no hauling fees, no sending his kids to school in Lampang Town, no paying down his debts, no more respect from anyone, completely dry in every way. To cut off the flow of this money was to cut off everything in his life. Often he recounted his woes, helplessly, to anyone who would listen. And he visited his sister every day as well. He had never borrowed from his sister before, and as he heatedly pointed out to her, she had rarely shared anything at all with him, ever. Finally she reluctantly gave him a ten-baht note to make him go away. That was about enough for a bottle of rice-grain alcohol. So Gongkam bought a bottle of it from his sister with the money she had just given him and was last seen storming off toward the cremation forest.

The next day, early in the morning, children on their way to school and monks on their way to alms were the ones who found Gongkam, dead and dangling from the cham chaa tree in the charnel ground.

Gothic Ethnography

That is not the end of the story of Gongkam. It is only getting started. There will be a ghost. And this, too, marks the ending of what may have seemed like it was going to be an ordinary enough ethnography about abstraction, immateriality, finance, and ghosts and the beginning of something else.

Because that is what is due, at least literarily if not intellectually: these relations between idea and matter, fiction and nonfiction, construction and reality, holding their formation throughout the marching, incremental progress of the conquest of the unknown by the known. Is allegiance to this fantasy ever unwarranted?

Great respect is due to the ontological turn in anthropology for its ingenious alternative to this question. To characterize this turn — if you can abide a sweeping simplification (and whether the ontological turn itself is a thing, I will not debate) — one could say that it has, among other things, sought the admission of ontologically inadmissible entities into narrow academic discourses in order to destabilize rigid ontological assumptions, open conversations, and disrupt academic business as usual. "Taking seriously" in this context has often meant to allow previously barred things to enter into participation with the seriousness of academic discourse (perhaps also secular materialist discourse). Academic discourse can admit into its menagerie of real things more real things to be taken seriously.

Seriousness has appeared to be central to the ontological turn in anthropology, prompting Tom Boellstorff, for one, to comment in his meditation on the digital real and the ontological turn that it is almost "conflating ontology with 'taking seriously.'"[6] To be sure, there are many ways in which to take things earnestly in anthropology that do not require specific kinds of ontological parity. But that is an easy out that Boellstorff does not take because it forecloses the productive avenues that the ontological turn provides for his work: destabilizations of the assumed difference between the digital as somehow unreal on the one hand and the so-called real world that is more real on the other.

One could also say that there are ways of taking certain things earnestly in the turn that have not necessarily equated to a demonstrable ontological shift. Yet this distinction between seriousness and ontology has even another possibility, which is not to question the ontology side of it so much as the seriousness side of it. This seriousness itself, its very form, literally as the performance of academic truth, is not as questioned and remains more stable. It is not like Viveiros de Castro and Phillipe Descola's thought—as writing—looks any different in form than any other standard anthropology. That is on purpose.

And if we just keep on this slight focus/emphasis on writing as such, then we might shift the interpretation a little bit toward what can be done with this: that the ontological turn's main disciplinary effect could be not so much to admit previously unacceptable entities into anthropology but to expand what could possibly count as acceptable writing.

Those two alternatives might sound as if they are almost the same thing, but they are not quite. In fact, the first — the admission of barred entities — is not so easy as it seems. It requires another kind of work, work that cannot easily or ever be done outside a recognition of and alteration in the medium.

Perhaps — and for now, let us just gently initiate this here, not insist, and merely follow up with the stories to come — there are other possible starting places than the earnest realism of anthropological discourse as a method of critical thought.

So, it is not a better starting place here but a different one: Why take spirits more seriously? Why not, instead, take less seriously the form of knowledge delineation and resultant image of what is real in academic writing?

This can start with nothing less than *recognizing writing as writing*. For example, need we really take seriously sentences like the following (published) ones?

> Forms of political power and influence created through the public re-definition of certain emotions in Thailand can be neither completely understood through local categories and conceptions nor can be accounted for as simply an extension of globalization, nor likewise can they be understood as simply assertions of local resistance nor an enfoldment into the global order of things. Instead, these rituals of national sentiment and value embody the power, tensions, and unstable points of opportunity for liberation and domination that are inherent in the phenomena of globalization.[7]

Leave it to an anthropologist to manage to write a lot that does not say a thing. And I was the one who wrote that (not that "I" means much here). Although the register of the prose is as reference to real things — as it is in many such sentences in anthropology — looked at carefully as writing, it is not really pointing to anything but conceptual creations, is it? Yet this can count as "serious" and is about the real simply by virtue of it being *written in the form that signifies the real.*

I realize this is a simple idea, yet strangely, I feel the need to pause here, because it seems sometimes that so many academics do not get this simple idea, or do not really take it in. There is a way of writing, of diction and syntax, that *itself* signifies the real, seriously. That is, it is not the referents that the content of writing is pointing to, whether understood naïvely as real things or understood as signified, but the form and style themselves that signify seriously realness.

Take this example, chosen almost at random and yet also so typical in prose style (but which may be more skillful than the previous example). Here, Karen Barad is positioning the aim of a project in distinction to the "linguistic turn" and to go beyond how, in the linguistic turn, "even materiality . . . is turned into a matter of language or some other form of cultural representation."[8] In other words, opposing the situation where "language has been granted too much power."[9] To simplify things quite a bit, it can be said that Barad is joining an ontological turn with an astute call for admitting an entity that seems to have been rendered inadmissible into scholarly discourse: matter itself! This is more interesting and pot-stirring, obviously, than the piece of my own text quoted above, which tells us more about dull routines than it does about ontology. Barad's text breaks a hole in the wall for others who are refugees from cultural construction, and in some ways this present text is in alignment with that. But while I would caution against founding anything on an unexamined belief in matter, and note that faith in matter is anything but in need of rescuing, I would not disagree about the turn from constructivism and cannot fault anything for its primary story concept. The point of the story is to bring this barred thing, "matter," back. Without that, there is no story. And so instead, it is specifically about ways of writing and reading themselves and their aims that I am wondering about in passages like the following:

> What is needed is a robust account of the materialization of all bodies — "human" and "nonhuman" — and the material-discursive practices by which their differential constitutions are marked. This will require an understanding of the nature of the relationship between discursive practices and material phenomena, an accounting of "nonhuman" as well as "human" forms of agency, and an understanding of the precise causal nature of productive practices that takes account of the fullness of matter's implication in its ongoing historicity.[10]

Wow. Is that all?

And remember, this text is calling for going beyond a "representationalism" that seeks to correlate words to reality.[11] Looked at in a certain way, as intended seriously, as a conquest of the unknown by the known and the transcendence of language in a project for precise understandings and robust accounting of "matter" that would be accurate about the workings of the processes and phenomenon named, present and accounted for, and which are presumed to actually exist . . . who wouldn't want all that? I would like some fries with that, too. And yet is this prose really up to the task of exiting from representationalism when it clearly borrows so heavily from its stylistics, departing from that style not one bit? Or, by contrast, is it academically required that it have this serious realness and will-to-knowledge, performatively, to launch a contestation?

But such prose could be read another way. This signification of serious realness through diction and syntax could also seem humorous in its reach, and ironically so given its position as "countering" a preoccupation with language and a critique of representationalism. What if, instead, we were to take it as a kind of sci-fi fantasy, intentionally wacky in its will to a thorough and direct knowledge: does it not now look kind of cool and funky?

Yet what seems to underlie the serious believing-in-its-own-thoughts of this literary form so common in the social sciences and anthropology is the tie to the performance of itself as a document of the real, expanding the territory or precision of our knowledge over the unknown or over the wrongly known things there. But rather than leaving the reference to the seriously real relatively intact as academic literary form, might one possible alternative — not a methodological requirement but a possibility — be to create a need to destabilize these forms of writing themselves?

What follows, therefore, is a twisted-reality balance that might shift the attention to a somewhat different reach, in this case for spirits. And in this case it is a question of how to work with these spirits as more — or at least differently — than either merely as a source of metaphor to be extracted in social theory's service, or "granted" a realness or seriousness whose status is officially stamped in the currency of social theory's own forms of knowledge and value.

Perhaps, for now, we could think of this as an *in-between* — a subject upon which Derrida and other writers of ghosts have alighted upon with some enthusiasm: the category of the specter provides an ontological-like category that hovers between being and nonbeing, real and unreal, present and absent. Not quite ontological but hauntological.

Perhaps nowhere is the drawing upon the spirit world for inspiration more curious than in Derrida's essays on justice and Marx, where there has been a strange flicker, like a sudden switch to photographic negative, in the notion of hauntology. It starts with Marx's "spectropoetics," as Derrida called it: the fairly constant availing of images, tropes, words, drawn from the Victorian literatures of ghosts, spirits, phantasms, revenants, werewolves, and vampires, all recollected in *Specters of Marx*.[12] For although Derrida does take these with tongue in cheek, as they seem to have been meant by Marx, he moves toward something greater in his contemplation of this inheritance, that the image and economy of ghosts are not merely tropological and, instead, that inheritances of past injustice are manifest in ghosts as a kind of trace-like presence of the call of justice that we can neither accept nor discard and instead need to learn to *live with*, which is not a question of law or human right, but of responsibility, that in order to live, we must learn from the dead. What justice do ghosts require?

"So it would be necessary to learn spirits," as Jacques Derrida has said of hauntology:

> To learn to live with ghosts, in the upkeep, the conversation, the company, or the companionship, in the commerce without commerce of ghosts. To live otherwise, and better. No, not better, but more justly. But with them. No being-with the other, no socius without this with that makes being-with in general more enigmatic than ever for us. And this being-with specters would also be, not only but also, a politics of memory, of inheritance, and of generations.[13]

Pay particular attention to the qualification in the last words here, almost ungrammatical in English translation, *"not only but also."* We see the trace of this most important carefulness that is so easily skipped over: not to override the being-with via an absorption into a prefabricated grid of political consciousness. Being-with specters is *not only* a politics of memory, inheritance, and generations and cannot be reduced to that.

It would be easy enough, I suppose, to dismiss the shift to hauntology in Derrida as disingenuous, that where Derrida means to emphasize the importance to be with and relate to spirits, what he really means is to extract from spectral tropoii some abstract, neither/nor conceptual category standing for philosophical indeterminacy within deconstruction. I can't fully disagree with that interpretation. For instance, as Colin Davis has put it, minimally:

Hauntology is part of an endeavour to keep raising the stakes of literary study, to make it a place where we can interrogate our relation to the dead, examine the elusive identities of the living, and explore the boundaries between the thought and the unthought.[14]

A fair enough aspiration, and no doubt valid to the source, yet potentially too easy and welcome for uptake. If *Of Grammatology* was where a recognition of writing became the deconstruction of philosophy, then hauntology might be simply a kind of modified and softened adjustment to this critique of the metaphysics of presence and its nihilistic potentials, a kind of not-quite-presence that works as a safety valve to release the nihilist pressure such that, in the end, there really is no other call beyond deconstruction except perhaps to a sort of academic conformity to radical common sense about current events.[15]

Not that it has not been taken that way. Fredric Jameson, widely quoted on this, was careful to insist that hauntology had nothing to do with whether or not one believes in ghosts (for instance, quoted in Colin Davis precisely to accomplish the function of drawing the implications safely back to an abstract notion of indeterminacy and uncertainty):

Spectrality does not involve the conviction that ghosts exist or that the past (and maybe even the future they offer to prophesy) is still very much alive and at work, within the living present: all it says, if it can be thought to speak, is that the living present is scarcely as self-sufficient as it claims to be; that we would do well not to count on its density and solidity, which might under exceptional circumstances betray us.[16]

The spectral is now expertly and safely diffused into nearly nothing. Phew!

A close call, yet not a foreclosure exactly either. Hauntology has lived on, eagerly embraced in at least some quarters in literary studies not only for the authorial trace of Derrida but because it became apparent that the idea of ghosts could have an important role in how one might mediate the understanding of writing and texts with an openness to that which exceeds fossil knowledge.

One exemplar of this literature, one of many, is Elizabeth Loevlie's "Faith in the Ghosts of Literature,"[17] which is as clear as any other in finding in fictional writing a natural place where being-with spirits becomes possible, and the unspeakable can be spoken without the conviction of ontology precisely because "literature, unlike our everyday, referential language, is not obliged to refer to a determinable reality, or to sustain meaning."[18] Moreover, in a certain sense literature is not only a medium for hauntological presences but is itself the epitome of such — literature, so the argument goes, is precisely hauntological in its nature because of its traffic in nonpresent presences. We can

> explore literature as mode that invites and permits us to relate to and experience these haunting aspects of our human existence. I understand literature as a specific use of language through which the ineffable and unthinkable can, paradoxically, "speak." Here language strangely releases those spectres of life that other modes of discourse repress, exclude or simply fail to grasp. Literature moves us because it offers the unheard testimony of the unspeakable.[19]

Yet such approaches to Derrida in literature are, in effect, an easy out precisely because "literature" or "fiction" becomes classed as separate from realist text, such as social science, for example, which would presumably adhere to the frame of "everyday, referential language." The point is well made that literature allows for an "ontological quivering," as Loevlie puts it, following Maurice Blanchot,[20] and expresses what these referential discourses do not. Were we to apply this analysis to anthropology, for instance, this divide would therefore posit social science as "obliged to refer to a determinable reality," and then the divide itself is left untouched via the specialness of fiction. But these special roles for literature leave aside the deeper questioning that Derrida poses to realism and philosophy, indeed therefore also to anthropology, as to the assumption that in writing, as such, there is a "there" there, a there present, questioning that the referential language is stable *anywhere* in the ways it is imagined to be, and not merely in fiction, and what implications for writing result. Literature, defined in this way, as a special case, does not go far enough as hauntology.

Ghostly Matters

> It seemed to me that radical scholars and intellectuals knew a great
> deal about the world capitalist system and repressive states and yet
> insisted on distinctions — between subject and object of knowledge,
> between fact and fiction, between presence and absence, between
> past and present, between present and future, between knowing and
> not-knowing — whose tenuousness and manipulation seem precisely
> to me in need of comprehension and articulation, being themselves
> modalities of the exercise of unwanted power.
> — AVERY GORDON, *Ghostly Matters*

For all that literary fiction, held as distinctly separate, reveals about writing, writers, texts and haunting, that does not necessarily impact directly the implications of the disciplinary divides in knowledge. And this is where Avery Gordon's *Ghostly Matters* differs, perhaps, by arguing for absorbing literary sensibilities of haunting into the social sciences themselves. This accomplishes what may be a more destabilizing move as a literary register and is deliberately theorized in *Ghostly Matters*, which starts with a simple enough social fact: the fact that haunting is

> a constituent element of modern social life. . . . Neither premodern superstition nor individual psychosis: it is a generalizable social phenomenon of great import. To study social life one must confront the ghostly aspects of it. This confrontation requires (or produces) a fundamental change in the way we know and make knowledge, in our mode of production.[21]

At a bare minimum: haunting, socially, is.

And it is a subject that sociology has no tools to comprehend. As such, it demands a methodology suitable to the fact of it. For Gordon the starting point, but certainly not ending point, is literary fiction, precisely because it "has not been restrained by the norms of professionalized social science, and thus it often teaches us, through imaginative design, what we need to know but cannot quite get access to with our given rules of method and modes of apprehension."[22]

Ghostly Matters was an attempt to rethink history and haunting that challenged both positivistic sociology and what at the time was called a "postmodernist" challenge to positivism. It is a different interest in the specialness of literature as a realm unpoliced by disciplinary enforcement of the real and from which the positivist social sciences can be informed or impacted.

By contrast, sociology's birth, as Gordon points out, literally entailed distinguishing itself from literature, and in its early times sociology was quite consumed with the defenestration of literature from itself, even if its subject matter itself confronts "cultural imaginings, affective experiences, animated objects, marginal voices, narrative densities, and eccentric traces of power's presence."[23] Yet, as a mode of storytelling, it is precisely defined by its not being any of those things and has historically arrived at a novel claim: "to find and report the facts expertly." Sociology and related disciplines found their disciplinary boundary precisely around maintaining a disciplinary object, "social reality," according to the distinction of what is socially real and true, thus doing the work to distinguish what is really going on from what is wrongly understood. In other words, dispelling social fictions. "The capacity to say 'This is so.'"[24]

In sociology, as it is in anthropology, what connects all its subjects in intricate webs is a story while, at bottom, what is striven for is the truth. Gordon identifies this contradiction and highlights that the facing of it is elided by policing creativity and by maintenance of the obligatory signification of not-fiction in academic prose.

As Gordon takes haunting to also be an expression of past wrongs and injustices, then rethinking history in terms of literary haunting shares potential common causes with social science, and yet this is where the analysis hardens around the interpretation of ghosts as expressions of the large-scale, abstract social and historical forces: "the ghost is just a sign" of haunting that has taken place, with haunting taken to be something vaster, "a social figure."[25]

The status of the real in haunting is mediated for Gordon because of a practical sociological impasse — broad historical and political dynamics and structures play themselves out in ambiguous and complex ways, exceeding the thoughts we have about those structures. Thus, sociology and all similar disciplines are "troubled by the contrast between conceptual or analytical descriptions of social systems and their far more diffused and delicate effects."[26]

It is in the ambiguities and complexities of everyday life, haunting perhaps paramount among them, that we can find another way to read back into those structures: "In haunting, organized forces and systemic structures that appear removed from us make their impact felt in everyday life in a way that confounds our analytic separations and confounds the social separations themselves."[27]

In a sense it is precisely haunting itself that proves these "organized forces" and "systemic structures" more real by making manifest their presence.

And yet, as a practice of writing, Gordon realizes that attention to ghostly matters allows us the possibility to "fill in the content differently." And that means, necessarily, a different relationship to writing, found first but not last in literature: "to find in writing that knows it is writing as such lessons for a mode of inscription that can critically question the limits of institutional discourse."[28]

In Writing That Knows It Is Writing as Such

Might the signification of not-fiction in the prose form of anthropology act as a refusal to write and think as though writing is writing? (The other obvious culprits being reviews, standard formulas, and a kind of gate keeping and policing.)

Remarkably, there has been little uptake of hauntology in anthropology despite anthropology's occasional attention to writing form and despite its anything-but-mild interest in ontological openness coming only a few years after Derrida's hauntological turn.

I suspect that one key difference between anthropology's recent ontological openness and hauntology is that anthropology's ontological openness has an emphasis on admissibility rather than inadmissibility, knowing rather than not-knowing. Perhaps in deconstruction there is something almost too destabilizing, for the metaphysics of presence running through the prose of anthropology would, of course, lean ontologically toward copresence (ontological parity) or simultaneous presence (multiple worlds) rather than toward "writing as such." What renders Derrida's approach different is precisely all the deconstructive thought of decades before, where it can hardly be argued that anything else dreamed of in Horatio's philosophy is any more "here" or "there" than the specter or than the assumptions of material presences and of actual, existing writers who are themselves actually existing entities speaking to actually existing entities.

To be sure, it is an almost perfectly valid reading to see the specter in Derrida as merely a metaphorical extraction from the spirit world, and I still do not know whether I do not think this as well: the force of secular materialist commonsense feels strong in him. And so then the French intellectual finds the perfect category to occupy a needed slot in his discourse, surprise, surprise. The specter in that case serves the purposes of a concept that captures indeterminacy and a certain inadequacy, that is, an inability to use current analytics to adequate, to accurately point to something that lies in between the self-evident categories that seem to be at hand, such as that between the living and the dead, the human and nonhuman, time and being, past and future, and so on. But this use of metaphors and topoi of the spirit world would remain merely tropological when the self-evident task — to declare an accurate and adequate analysis of reality, and/or the impossibility of doing so — remains somehow on the front burner, or, we could also say, to the extent that it does. But clearly that is not the point with Derrida.

A mere tropological spectral writing takes metaphors from the spirit world to, as it were, complete its thoughts about what exceeds its grasp. Or it sees haunting as standing for something else that is actually real: ghosts are merely signs, emblems of social anxiety or some such, which are more real than ghosts and which emanate out of structural historical processes that are even more real than that. Tropological spectralism dashes its concepts with images of ghosts and sprinkles the writing with similes of the supernatural. Tropological spectralism sustains an intonation of not-really-meaning-it-yet-sort-of-meaning-it-but-not-really-ness. We write about ghosts, but, of course, *they are not, and we are*. The tropological becomes a kind of cushion or a kind of throwing-your-hands-up at the inadequacy of representational language, a kind of supplemental acknowledgement that allows the writing business to go on as usual; on the one hand there is that which can be represented, and on the other hand there is that which cannot be represented and for which we use metaphor, art, poetry, literature, and ghosts.

But when the adjustment and correction of referential knowledge to reality is not the deliberative task in the writing, which is to say, when that is not the goal, the game changes. A metaphysics of presence presumes that there is a subject, a separately existing writer who views through the partial constructor of language a partial view on a reality that is also out "there," however incompletely known, perhaps to refine that knowledge and get the language to line up.

In an interview, "On 'Madness,'" Derrida is asked, then, "Why is it so important to write?"

> The self does not exist, it is not present to itself before that which engages it in this way and which is not it. There is not a constituted subject that engages itself at a given moment in writing for some reason or another. It is given by writing, by the other: born ... by being given, delivered, offered, and betrayed all at once. . . . Saint Augustine speaks often of "making the truth" in a confession. . . . I try, by citing him often, to think how this truth rebels against philosophical truth — a truth of adequation or revelation.[29]

It is difficult to emphasize enough that this means to say that the writer does not preexist the text. This has been, of course, something far more assimilated to literary studies than it has been in anthropology, where the question of the ethnographer — the one who has perceived and thought the knowledge created — is not inquired into as to its ontological status. But is there a "there" there in the ethnographer? Does the ethnographer speak?

By contrast, it is not as far of a critical leap for the theorist of literature to identify fiction as a mirror of the sourceless source of the text, that there is an "affinity between the sacred speech of the oracle and the potentially literary voice that emerges through what is written because none of them originate in the speaking subject," as Loevlie puts it, drawing upon Blanchot here:

> Like sacred speech, what is written comes from no one knows where, it is authorless, without origin, and hence, refers to something more original. Behind the written word, no one is present, but it gives voice to absence, just as in the oracle where the divine speaks, the god himself is never present in his speech, and it is the absence of god that speaks then.[30]

Yet this makes a certain kind of sense only inside a referential world where bodily presences, oracles, are taken to be what is meant by "present" and a god as something "absent." In such a view spirits would never speak, only mediums would, because "to speak" is then tied to a subject position that is, in turn, tied to the metaphysics of sound vibrations of the body. But we could see the text as an embodiment of a voice that is originless in the sense that a writer is not a present thing. This not only includes the author but the addressee as well, a function of the code and mark in writing itself, as Derrida put it in "Signature, Event, Context":

> All writing, therefore, to be what it is, must be able to function in the radical absence of every empirically determined addressee in general. And this absence is not a continuous modification of presence; it is a break in presence, "death," or the possibility of the "death" of the addressee, inscribed in the structure of the mark.[31]

This is, for Derrida, true of *all* writing, for writing "to be what it is" and therefore both the same as and exceeding the point in Loevlie's accounting of Toni Morrison's *Beloved*, a point that is more narrowly hauntology inspired:

> What Morrison's text demands from its readers is that they have faith in the ghosts of literature. And to have this faith is to be smitten with the quivering ontology of that in which we believe. In *Beloved* this spectrality is more tangible as one of the main characters is a ghost. However, and here I recall Blanchot, every great text has its center of unreadability, its spectrality. Literature is the release of this middle zone, this in-between, that haunts us all. So to read literature is to be exposed to the hauntology of the text, and thereby to one's own spectrality. In what sense am I? What is it to exist? Where do I end and does the other start? How does the death of others, and my own death, haunt me? How can I live with the knowledge of all that I can never know?[32]

As an appraisal confined to literature rather than all writing, this is almost too readily acceptable, yet a certain instability opens because obviously these questions are not merely the questions of literature, at least not for Derrida or Gordon. These questions can bleed into other genres. Perhaps the spectral nature of the writer emerges more visibly in what is being classed as literature simply because the spectrality of the text and writer is precisely that which is most studiously averted from recognition in the referential text. There is far less suspension because the referential text tells "seriously true" stories, evoking faith in its seriously meant language in ways that pass under the radar, leaving the spectrality of the text, and of the writer and the reader for that matter, unreflected. This is the seriousness of referential text seen precisely not as the writing that it is.

Not that such text always should be seen as writing in this sense, nor even that it frequently should be. It is not the common and laudable aim of anthropological discourse to address the seriousness of issues that I want to be skeptical about. It is instead about how the particular way anthropological discourse itself purports to be taken seriously, at least as literary form. In other words it is not what we might call the world that we might not take seriously but the way knowledge of it is performed that might be looked at, occasionally, as somewhat fictional and also maybe even strangely comical that it could be taken as seriously true. And this is not to say that what I propose here is a cure but merely a different attitude and a different starting point.[33]

What I propose here is something more approaching the nature of the Gothic, or to be more exact, it is at play with the Gothic. A Gothic ethnography might involve, like the common definition of Gothic literature, both the approaching sense of a supernatural world that is seemingly — but not quite — lost by a (falsely) imagined "modernity," and the fundamental subversion of modernist imagination by the return of unassimilated entities that defy and confound the new order, rendering the modern strange and irreal and exposing its incomplete vision of the world, if only in story.

Unfortunately, for reasons beyond my control, I cannot honestly say that Gothic ethnography, like Gothic fiction, is all story, however. The separation of functions between fiction and referential language cannot be observed, because what writing is cannot be apparent only in some texts and not others. Gothic ethnography here does not exclude the "true story" as conventionally understood. It is less complete than fiction, an incomplete vision, including mistakes about who is, and what it is to be, alive; who is, and what it is to be, dead; who is person and who is spirit; who is narrator, character, and writer; and a stream of other indefinite entities that definitely do not necessarily exclude real ghosts in the most literally simple senses of the terms "real" and "ghost."

When one already knows where to put each thing, each in its place, this is to give up all possibility, as in the nouny social science that fixates process into its nouns through the izationization of language and the assignment of classificatory schemes. There can be no easy classification scheme in a Gothic ethnography: Would a true Gothic social science suddenly reveal, in a twist at the end, that the realist narrator who described the true forces of globalization was, in fact, a robot programmed to create social science and that in the end it all was a constructed fiction? Or would it instead take the reader on a fantastic, seemingly fictional journey requiring the suspension of disbelief only to reveal in the end that it was all in fact a true story?

Or is it social-science-as-usual itself that is already committing the sin of false, uncanny fiction as Freud identified it?[34] Which is to say it might be like those "true stories" that Freud felt so begrudged about, where a supernatural account is told as if it were true and is meant to be taken seriously as reference and representation of what was real, thus creating an uncanny chill in the reader, because of the belief in it being real, only to reveal disappointingly at the end that it was all made up. As disciplines progress and new research and new methods and debates reveal the past chapters in the advance of the known over the unknown as false, are we not being strung along in a similar story, much like the false uncanny, induced to believe and then realizing later it was made up in the end?

Derrida said we must speak with specters. And others tell us these specters are not seriously real of course. Of course not. Don't worry. You can read on. Derrida is not doing anything freaky.

Nothing out of place.

I said just now that I propose a play with Gothic ethnography, and yet that word "propose" is funny in that it almost implies that I am in a writer's lab coat, exploring an experimental method — "experimental ethnography" is something I have put on my cv — that you can now build upon in the future to move the discipline forward, expand the conquest of the unknown by the known, or increase the precision of our apprehension of it. But if one looks a little askew at this, with different eyes, perhaps eyes also attuned to literary form, could that all-too-common performance of revealing the brand-new modus for future anthropological knowledge not also appear at times to be the true anthropological cheese factor?

What if, instead of expanding what is known over the unknown, the light of the known realm itself is changed, sharing in something like what can happen in fiction or in Gothic fiction or in the brand-new anthropological method — which other anthropologists may now commence doing — of gothic ethnography?

Or not. Everything back in its place. All voices placed in their empirically real, discursive positionality, which is not a fiction. Identities fixed in the discursive grid. Authors are limited to express themselves within what their discursive positionality permits, and this positionality is real. We know who each person is on the historic grid and what each being is and, last but not least, this means also that we already know what *being* is. No mixing. No excesses. Everything in its place.

This is what I'm chanting to myself as I suddenly feel destabilized by these thoughts and as other voices enter in unbidden, ventriloquists taking over my inner voice. I'm not myself. Much like Descartes's *Meditations* at his fireside, as he intentionally imbibes his designer drug of doubt, I'm feeling out of sorts. Images of Gongkam's suicide are dancing in my brain, although I already know it is not his death that really matters so much as what happened to Gongkam, and to everyone, and even to me, after his death. Things are breaking up.

> If he loves justice at least, the "scholar" of the future, the "intellectual" of tomorrow should learn it and from the ghost. He should learn to live by learning not how to make conversation with the ghost but how to talk with him, with her, how to let them speak or how to give them back speech, even if it is in oneself, in the other, in the other in oneself: they are always there, specters, even if they do not exist, even if they are no longer, even if they are not yet. They give us to rethink the "there" as soon as we open our mouths.[35]

I'm losing it, but some voice inside me is telling me, "Let it happen: just lie back and think of multi-sited ethnography."

Faces in the Water

Gongkam was, in fact, my uncle, or "second uncle" I guess you call it in English. I know this vocabulary not because I know much English, or studied English much, but because I have access to the knowledge of my host, who is a native speaker of English: everything he knows, I know (it's more complicated than simply that, but I will leave that for later). Still, we did, as children, learn the English word "uncle," but I think we thought it meant the same thing that we mean in Thai; really any man not too old and not too young we would call "uncle" on the street in the village as a sign of respect and acknowledgment of our connection as fellow people. I only have vague memories of Gongkam, but my host knows more from asking around (he asks around a lot), and between the two of us, I get a very vivid picture of a sad story that doesn't seem to end. It's a complicated story, just as is the means by which it is possible to tell it. Let's just say for now that this isn't my first language. Nor is this my first host; far from it. I'm a ventriloquist, you could say, and more: I have the run of the body of his memories and his language, awkward, intellectual constructions as they are. There's no good way for me to put it because his words and images and style of speaking and thought and sense of audience and this language are all foreign to me, and although I use his style and am in control, it also sometimes feels as though it's not me who is speaking.

I am myself, however, very much a part of the story, which is not only about how my life's course was forever impacted by that one act of my uncle. It's also about how we can know the connection of the courses of all of our lives to the courses of all of our deaths, about the balances of account columns and lack of them between this world and the next.

For me, the seeing of this began when I was a young girl growing up in Northern Thailand. I was drawn to solitude in the quietest places. In that sense, I was quite unlike the other girls and boys I grew up with, and indeed quite un-Thai, at least given what we were taught in school by the Bangkok curriculum about our nature as selfless and generous and in constant communal connection with our family, neighbors, and nation. Maybe there could be no one less Thai than me.

When I was a girl, we didn't have toys from the store. We made our own out of sticks and dirt and rocks and cans or waded in the stream and the creek that is now long dried and where once in a while one of us would die, drown, disappearing forever under the murky brown water to live almost forever there in a memory but also as a ghostly part of the world, part of the world's force, embedded in the banks, in the clammy silt clay that startles at the first touch of your foot, sending a rippling shudder up your legs and all around the surface of your skin, the exact analogue in the physical world of being brushed by a spirit. I myself was always drawn to the water, to the creek, and in the latter days of my childhood I'd often seek out the creek alone, when solitude was not a state that most Thai kids in those days sought. We loved to be together and knew no other life than that of the peripatetic band of children assembling in the tangled well-worn paths between houses, where we coursed as the lifeblood of the village through its veins of alleys rather than shipped off down straight grids like the kids of today's planned settlements. But for some reason, I was different and sought out the solace and would hurry off, without my mother knowing it, down to the creek, where I would steal a boat and paddle and drift off on the quiet surface. Have you ever heard nothing, absolutely nothing but a silence broken by the eddy of a paddle gently cutting and kissing the water? It seems unnatural, but the mind is like that. There can be a chorus of bugs and birds out there, but you hear only the one thing. It lulls you into peace. And in that calm, I knew that my friends and former playmates, and those of my father and mother's time as well, lay somewhere down below me, hungry for my company. Somehow that didn't disturb me from the singular sound of water and its partner, silence

that eased my mind and filled me with the bare and ordinary presence of the world.

Sometimes I was caught when I made my way home and was given a good slap with my father's switch for putting my life at risk. But getting caught happened far less than my parents could have dreamed was possible. I was hard to find out and hard to catch, a skinny, boyish girl who nevertheless hated boys and would constantly get into fights with them, which I won every time. I was a wriggly baby and then a bony spider-girl who only stopped moving when alone and in peace. Those were the moments that would stay with me and linger on long after they were gone. I can't tell you how much I miss that world, the feel of old wood on your feet, on your bottom, in your hands. The paddle so present in your hands, and yet there was an unsensed chaos of green grass and fiery ants waiting on the bank. Janpen was my name at the time (later I got really sick, and to fool the spirits, my name was switched to Anchalee). Janpen, "Full Moon." Like the night I was born and also like the tint of my world and feelings, always a little cool, a little unreal. A moon-child, paddling through the creek a little too late, a little later than I should have.

The dusky light coated the surface of the water while the tallest trees still prickled with the gold light of day's end. That was when the first one came to me.

It was the up in that tree by the bank, the one my mother told me never to go near.

"That is the Tree Woman's place," she would say. "Don't go there, or she'll get you, hit your mind and possess your body."

But I was curious, so I kept looking, and up in the tallest branches, there was one that was glowing, bright white. I felt no fear, exactly, but still there was a weakness and sinking in my belly that made it difficult to even find the strength to move a muscle let alone wield the paddle. But I was drifting in the light current and passed under the branch. When I was far enough away, I could paddle again. I headed straight home.

But now my eyes darted to the eddy of the paddle. As I flicked past it, I turned my head, and in the expanding ripple on the surface was the reflection of a face. A boy's face, white as boiled rice, big black eyes desperately glaring at me. Again, the next stroke, another face, another boy, crying and angry, as if it were my fault. A girl, then a baby, everywhere I stuck the paddle in the water was another figure. I could not stop from looking, but the faster I paddled, the faster I passed them by. The faster I wanted to go, the faster I paddled, and the more faces appeared. Until the whole creek behind me was a wake of the lost faces of children, and now my heart was beating so fast, and my breath heaved in my chest.

I turned for the bank and crashed into it. I leaped from the boat, and one foot hit the bank while the other foot sunk in the clammy mud and stuck. I wasn't sure whether it was a hand or the mud that had hold of me up to the ankle. The feeling of the silty hand closing on me filled me with a superhuman strength, and I wrenched it free and ran off in a frantic hobble with one heavy foot that took far too long to shed the remnants of mud.

Later, when I got home, it didn't take long for everyone to figure out that I was responsible for the lost boat that had drifted away. I got the switch and good. But that wasn't the worst thing that happened that night. My neighbor, the man next door, became possessed by the Tree Woman that very same night. She announced herself, and he spoke in her voice, howling all night and keeping me up and scared to death of falling asleep.

Eventually, I did drift off to sleep. And by the time I woke up, he was dead.

I was very sad for him but also relieved. He had once tried to corner me all alone in a room in his house, but I had escaped. I kept it quiet back then, just as I have until now, while everyone tried to find the meaning of the possession, to figure out how and what had happened and why, when I knew who it was that had caused the Tree Woman to come out of the forest to hit his mind and seize his body. They pondered, in fear and wonder, what it meant that the tree would steal his body and then take his life.

Horror Stories

Even the face disappears and only the number remains, virtually without form . . . and therefore a freed human imagination could have the power of return, to insert itself into the very fabric of the most utilitarian aspects of human exchange, and stake its claim.

Note, however, that in Adam Smith's horror story the encroachment of human imagination into the symbolic order of utility is not merely an alien invasion of fabulations, as Smith consciously portrays it, but could also be conceived as an incursion of a real desire, desire animating ever-expanding realms of trade and value, incursions into a utilitarian realm from which it has been fantastically imagined as banished and inadmissible by the barrier of Euro-enlightenment reason, which, it is no small secret, functions also (though in no way referenced in Smith's text) to imagine the barrier between the living and the dead.

What I want to know, and what I cannot get my . . . er . . . let us for now call her my "friend" . . . to tell me, is how ghosts and spirits take hold of numbers (as they most often do these days). In thinking through and negotiating a life in postcrashing Thailand, there is hardly a sense in which the resounding effects of globalized, digitized, abstract value do not permeate everyday life, and yet that life has for a very long time already fully resonated with an interest in other abstract realms of existence, alternative immaterialities to which, it will be argued, our attention can be turned to considerable benefit. The two realms, ghosts and numbers, seem ordained, each to the other, especially among those number players who seek insider information from the next world.

The association of ghosts and numbers can be an unsettling way to think about the settled common sense that we face an increasing abstraction of economy and the virtualization of finance transactions and all the implications that this has on the conduct of our social life, the organization of what has been called capital, and the proliferation of situations of broad disparity in access to the realms of financial power. Are the realms of abstract capital splitting off from what appear to be material relations and taking on a life of their own (an impossible horror in Marxist thought, a possible horror in classical economics), or is abstraction simply the tip of an iceberg of real social relations, which it reflects and embodies, represents and proxies? In this situation of heightened freakiness, one might be tempted to remain in awe of this realm and grant it an ontological presence that is equivalent to that of any other thing in this world.

The realism embodied in theory stories of fear and awe of this realm are disturbing in many ways, and on purpose, in the way that realism calls forth the sense of an impending and looming ethereal monster of digitization that could swallow the world, in the sense of a relentless logic that will lead the world through an increasingly momentous spiral, its horror most especially defined by the way that immaterial logic separates us from materiality and real limits, and yet has very real impacts on our mortal coils, such as on the oil that burns, the air that is breathed, and even in stirrings in the genetic calm that still settles over all the species of the planet but may erupt into yet another abstract force beyond our control; the number leads our minds away from the earth and from our bodies as though we are possessed. And the limit of material return on this matter is its fraternal-twin monster, the twin to the monster of abstraction.

And yet . . . our question of ghosts and numbers here will be different, a more twisted look at this, the conventional equation between mind and matter outlined above. Certainly, there is something spiritually suggestive and suggested by the wires, cables, and wireless transmissions as they carry invisible forces that generate a realm that is analogous, at least, with the animated energy of an immaterial existence. All notional values are given a life that is so powerful, so compelling, and the thought that we would be commanded by their imperatives is, in a way, an assertion that we can create spirits that possess us, not just the notion of spirits but ones with a certain kind of reality to them as well. We can give life to our dreams, and our dreams can take life, form. And this metaphorical flight can all make sense as long as we remain more or less in the imaginary of the anthropological point of view — which is to say, the imaginary not necessarily of a discipline called anthropology but of a reading stance that depends upon the suspension of disbelief and a view through the lens of "culture," where things are both agnostically true and agnostically not at the same time. In that imaginary, this is as close as one can come to a discourse of ghosts and numbers. And that is why, perhaps, the image of the specter proliferates tropologically now, just as it did in Marx.

Ground down in some Marxist sensibilities is the lesson that the money form has an animated spirit that arises from a specific and very real locality: from the sacrifice of qualitative value to quantitative value in the sacrifice of labor, which lets loose the fetish of value, which then propels the very real realm of abstract exchange.

This is the spirit of capital and the animated spiritual substance let loose from a prior and secret, or at least secreted, violence. But there are two products, are there not? The fraternal twin to the commodity fetish is the very real class of people produced by this process, which cannot be revoked. That is to say, the force that animates the realm of abstract capital is the same force that is assembling itself, seeking itself out, gathering from fragments and amassing into a wholly new specter, the "spectre haunting Europe" of the *Communist Manifesto*, a singular specter that will overpower this strange animism. It is not simply that Marx sees the capitalists as having inferior insight into the nature of reality. There is a very real connection between the abstract values of capital and actual sacrifices made on the level of the exchange of qualitative value for quantitative capital, of work for labor power. Human sacrifice.

But could a gothic ethnography be a fantastic response to this speculative capitalist spectral tropoii, or would it only represent another expression of the pagan order of commodity fetishism?

All truth is a social construction, except for this sentence.

All truth is a social construction, including this sentence.

⚔ The first one, "all truth is a social construction, except for this sentence, which is not a socially constructed truth but a Truth that masters all other truths," was the unbelievable truth that they tried to teach him before I got my, as it were, hands on him.

My own story is, I know, just as hard to swallow as these strange learned swigs. I didn't know what to think at the time, or about the time, of this story either. I'm not even sure I believed it then, nor now, despite what happened.

But I was definitely, without doubt, frightened. Now there were two dead, my uncle Gongkam and the neighbor man, whose name always escapes me. I felt it all had something to do with me. I was a child, and that is what a child thinks of the things that go on around her.

At night I had to keep the shutters closed no matter how hot it got in the summer. Even just a crack of moonlight in my window would cause me to awake in the night. After the Tree Woman came for the neighbor man and left, I began to have other strange visits. Even talking about the visits is uncomfortable, and I feel as though the world will open its folds again and drown me again with all those presences again.

Well, it started in the moonlight in my bed. At the foot of my bed I would see a tiny childlike figure, the size of a rat, crawling on all fours toward me. It was all yellow and glowed. It had a little child's face with a big smile, which made me smile at first until I saw that the grin did not move. Just one smile, always the same, and it had no eyes, just spots of black nothing for eyes, crawling on all fours toward me, smiling, smiling. I screamed and woke up the whole house and spent the rest of the night with *mae* and *paw* even though I was a bit too old for that. I cried whenever it came back so that I could go to bed with mae and paw.

That was the first crack, when I was very tiny, and it is one of my earliest memories. There would be more later.

That was when the numbers started coming to me. That was when my mother began to latch on to me the way I latched on to her. She wanted the numbers, and I wanted to be near her forever. It worked out for both of us. She would ask me for numbers and then bet on the last two or three numbers in the black-market lottery.

Somehow, I was right half the time.

It didn't last my whole life. Mae told me that eventually a child grows up to the point where she is no longer pure. She begins to understand winning and losing. She begins to take an interest in money. It's at that point that her vision becomes stained. But an innocent child with no idea what the numbers are for can announce numbers freely and without passing through the stain of consciousness. For luck in numbers and money, you always go to the small children.

But I felt differently. I always thought, and still kind of believe, that my encounters with these presences were instead what put the numbers in my mind. Perhaps it was just a coincidence, and yet living in my skin, I can't help but feel there was a real connection. And feeling the connection is the same thing as there being one.

I was not the only one having encounters. There were other dabblers. That's why the problems really started.

After the children and monks found Gongkam's corpse dangling from the cham chaa tree, the villagers came, and before noon, cut him down, lugged him deep into the forest, dug a hole in the ground, laid him down, covered him over, reemerged from the wood without looking back, and then hitchhiked to work at the sugar mill because they had missed the one company bus what with the suicide business.

Gongkam's family, my cousins and aunts and uncles, were finally convinced — by horrible stories of ghosts, of the intense violation that suicide represented, of how miserable and obsessed Gongkam must have been at the time of death — that it was best to leave the ghost out in the forest rather than bring the corpse to the home for proper rites. Gongkam's elder sister, now the senior figure of the family, had no reluctance at all about this, as it would avoid the expense of a funeral wake, which would at a bare minimum last three nights and to which she would be obliged to contribute.

Of course, even with Gongkam's body ferreted away in the woods, he was nevertheless all too present in the village — in the talk that ran wild of the suicide, of the horrible expression on Gongkam's face, of his strange behaviors, of debt and money, of his miserly sister, the last one to speak to him alive.

Others continued to speak to him after his death, though secretly. Taking him way out into the forest had apparently not worked. One night a local medium, a pleasant enough woman with a soft-spoken way about her, was approached by some gamblers, some of whom had been friends or acquaintances of Gongkam's. After calling out to and plying Gongkam's spirit with cigarettes and rum, the medium began to gag, choke, and dry heave and finally erupted with a howl, bringing Gongkam into her body, where he proceeded to beat his chest, sob, cry, and yell in anger, all in quick alternation. He was cold, cold. It was so dark. There was pain down the back of his neck. He was grasping at his neck, clawing at it. Sometimes screaming in pain with his palms pressed hard against his temple.

These are mostly the things Gongkam was doing or saying at first, or so I am told. It took a long time to get Gongkam out of this funk, to stop telling everyone how he was feeling, to get him to focus on them and their desires. They wanted Gongkam to come with them, be with them, hanging over their shoulders, when they went to funeral wakes and while they were gambling there. They wanted him to guide their hands to the right numbers, let them release their money to drop softly down upon the gambling mat, on the right numbers. "Come on," they pleaded. "You owe your buddies."

And what will you do for me?

"Liquor and cigarettes every time we win."

But what about my body? I am cold.

"We will come to get you if you help us. Come on, share your knowledge with us."

And what will you do about my elder sister?

People may say various things about what the gamblers' response to that question might have been. The nicer version is that they finally pleaded their way through it with other promises and convinced Gongkam to accompany them to funeral casinos and share his insights into the numbers. The other version of this story might — given what happened later — be evidence admissible in a murder trial.

People talk a lot. This whole story is based on talk, most of all mine. The more important fact, in general, about that night is that it was the reason the story didn't come to an end with the hasty burial. Because these guys could not be satisfied and so would not leave Gongkam to his terrible fate alone. And so, to what would become the great misfortune of Jai Village, Gongkam shared his fate with them, with everyone.

❧ Do you want to know what happened next? The numbers did not come easily, not without a price.

That price was to discover what I am. Which was the same thing as the death of me.

But before I can even begin to go into what I mean by the death of me, there are some things you need to know about what happens when value and spirits mix themselves up in the seeming alternatives of immaterial and material form. And to really get it, to really understand what I have to say, it is not going to be easy, not without a price. You are going to have to want it for yourself. Which is to say, you are going to have to want to partake in this death, if even only a little, and without knowing what it means. Which is to say that you need to start with desire, from a stance of desire and a look of desire. But desire for what?

A list of the objects that will appear here:

1 The description of a locale in Northern Thailand in several dimensions of memory and observation, including the context of global situations but by no means limited to, or even mainly, that.
2 Real ghost stories.
3 A terrible economic crash.
4 Money schemes of some variety.
5 Lottery.
6 Ghosts in global film, their distantly close hands.
7 The Nextworld, which can be divided into two subcategories:
   First, the realm of the afterlife and the beings beyond our dreamworld's thin barrier.
   Second, the ideas of spiritual animation that seize, and are seized by, those minds turned upon and enraptured by our dreamworld's orchestra of numbers in furious exchange and giving birth to an emergent future, those metaphors of spirit, which they use to call back down to earth the abstract beyond, or else to imagine, indefinitely and in delusion, that there will be no return.
8 Trees. Some with spirits.
9 A mirror. One in which you can see what you really are but not the kind you can hold in your hands.

These are just some of the things in this Nextworld, not necessarily the most important ones. I stopped at nine only because nine is the luckiest number in Thailand. Now I have mentioned that number three times, which is good because three is one-third of nine. But nine nines would be best, so now I have six, and three more to go to get off to a good start.

The word for nine is *gau* in Thailand, which is almost homonymous with the word for step and stepping forward and so represents forward momentum, progress, things getting better, advancement. Nine therefore is the most coveted number for birthdays, cell phone numbers, license plates, home addresses. Nine.

The things in an ethnography always exceed the capacity of the symbolic order of the reasonable everyday to satiate itself on full and final possession of them in its perception. To consider the consequences of this state of affairs in writing as such, however, cannot entail the stance nor the look of an objective realist lens. It is one thing to strike critical poses on the social construction of objective realism and its oppressive effects, which has been done with great fervor and repetition in scholarship. It is quite another thing to ask for something more than that.

To wake up through the social life of story is not to see through the mass fantasies, their ideological imaginary, and identify the desires, fears, and anxieties embedded and wedded to power. Is there something available that is even more resistant than such penetrating "insight"?

And so it is very much from the sidelines of the realist optic and frame that I will return us again, at long last, and feeling like we are ourselves again, to the end of things and the ardent attention of Kamnoi, sitting by her TV set, searching — and thus return to the ardent attention she places on the meaning of numbers in this life. There are countless realms in which she experiences a constant stream of imagery that can she can read back as displaced expressions of numerical values:

> Sometimes the numbers are there in the simplest of things. If I dream of a snake, that could be one. If it is "blue," that rhymes with two, if the snake slithers, then it is a five. Sometimes the dead, my father, mother, my ancestors, the place spirits, the Buddhist saints, or the lords of olden times appear with signs and symbols, or sometimes they speak the numbers. Sometimes I see car crashes, on TV or on the side of the road, and I note the number of dead, the number of vehicles, the license-plate numbers. Other times I see visiting dignitaries on TV or disasters at home or abroad. Everything that draws my attention could have a number lying within it.

For Kamnoi, finding the expression of winning lottery numbers is a constant interpretative endeavor of sorting through all apparitions of life, from satellite broadcasts circulating over the surface of the earth to dreams in the sleep of the night to the visitations by spirits and ancestors to strange occurrences appearing before the attention of everyday life.

Now one of the most remarkable things about such people who are so singularly focused on lottery is how lacking they are in elaborated consumerist fantasies about winning. When asked what she would do with a big lottery winning, Kamnoi's answers are remarkably mundane and mirror those of hundreds of others: she would buy a house for her children, pay for their schooling and that of her grandchildren. Asking questions about winning big in the lottery will not get one very far into anyone's fantasy life. All the mental work is turned instead, rather purely, toward interpretation of the numbers themselves. And it is here, in what may at first glance appear to be an elaborated work of fantasy in the realm of numbers, that we can begin to unbalance the equation of realism and fantasy we started with.

Imagine a life where you will do almost nothing without first making sure the numbers add up, that it is the right day, the right time, to buy a new motorbike, get married, bless your new baby, change the color of your hair, or even leave the house and buy a chicken in the market. Where the phenomenal world is a constant stream and series of incidences, coincidences, codes, symbols, all representing a constant iteration and language of figures, an utterly digital world with a fortune insistently but unclearly present, just waiting for the right read-back from the apparent to its numerical substrate. Imagine a world where there is not a thing that cannot be the occasion to place a bet, and after finding suitable partners, one gambles constantly not only on lottery, football, and the closing stock market index number but also on how many people will walk through the door of the shopping mall in the next five minutes or how many grains of have stuck to my third finger; whatever is happening is always translatable into a numerical instrument on which to turn, and harness, the generator of fate, which is at the source of financial fortune, a moment-to-moment living with a felt consistency that occurs on a plane of relationship with numbers that is difficult for those who spend far less time reading it that way to fathom.

Is this the famed, promised, and feared penetration of the neoliberal regime of economic abstraction into the thoroughmost recesses of intimate life, most especially of fantasy life?

Tracking seamlessly between television images, incidents in daily life, sleep, and dreams, including all the world that is normally conceived of as real, all phenomena are equally susceptible to interpretation as, in effect, dream, in that all phenomena can be read back through the dreamwork of the fateful universe to the primary numbers lying behind and within its appearances. In the manifest content of what we call the real world, nothing is as it seems, and everything arrives instead predigitized into phenomenal form.

Kamnoi's derealization of the phenomenal world might be likened to a popular cinematic fantasy, that of *The Matrix*,[36] where the clear-seeing hero Neo ("the One") finally perceives the illusions of the Matrix as the displaced representations of what is, at base, a number stream, thus gaining freedom from and power over that world.

But, of course, it is very different in one supremely important respect. For the clear-seeing Neo, who sees through the digital fantasy and into the black box and wired base, the real is a very present counterground upon which is rooted his existence, his eye, and his brain. But, of course, in Kamnoi's digitized world of phenomenally manifesting numbers there is nothing that is not ultimately linked to fate and the number stream, to an immaterial beyond. All phenomena, which one might classify as either dream or reality, are equally manifestations of a dreamwork worked upon the base of numbers.

Quite awry from a passive reaction to the neoliberal dream- and nightmarescape, quite displaced from desperate clinging and desire to the world driving bizarre cultural behaviors that are manifestations, in the real, of primary socio-historical forces, living in a world of apparitions of numbers has less grit and pull, is less serious, and has less traction on the mind.

Consider the occasion, to cite only one example from her life, when world leaders from the United States, China, Japan, Russia, Venezuela, the entire twenty-one nations of the Asia-Pacific Economic Corporation (APEC) Pacific Rim, descended on Thailand for an elaborate spectacle and performance of a shining new and ethereal world of a global finance and investment utopian community hosted by the Thai national leader. As Kamnoi sits transfixed to the constant live-video feed, she is not imbibing the hegemonic dreamworld but looking for other significances, connecting with numbers in the same way she would if the APEC meeting were a natural disaster, act of terrorism, or car wreck on the side of the road.

Living a rather otherworldly life of numbers has done nothing to increase a sense that the hostile and fearful world out there will strike her down into poverty and longing and that she must join up with the dominant solutions offered. Nor is she ruled by the consumerist fantasies displayed on her TV set. This consumerist dream material does not create serious objects of desire but instead is an occasion to look for correspondences and displacements of the number stream. Thus, reading against the grain and back from the manifest content of the dominant fantasies to the unstable field of probabilities that underlies her phenomenal world, her looking awry at fantasy itself is perhaps a more thorough apperception and freedom than the realist optic.

And if that is fantasy (although I am not saying that it is), then perhaps anthropology should get a little less real.

For the whole matter is one of "testing reality," pure and simple,
a question of the material reality of the phenomena.
—SIGMUND FREUD, "The 'Uncanny'"

This World and Another

It may be unlikely that the ghosts of this world will ever see eye to eye,
wake up out of the service that they have been pressed into, the work they
have been performing in mediating the world's transition from analog to
digital existence. It is unlikely that the ghosts of this world will ever unite,
even in film, where they do so much of their labor. And yet the least I can
do is use *Ethnography # 9* to call their attention to the global situation and
hope for the best.

And how I will begin to attempt this here is not so much with an over-
view of the situation but with a series of uncanny correspondences. These
all have something to do with the relations between apparently different mass-media and ethnographic realities, in particular how media play
themselves out on what could be called the ground level of ethnographic
analysis, what is sometimes called the "real world." This is, of course, quite
a problematic distinction between media and ground, between a realm of
representation, contrivance, fiction, on the one hand, and the real world,
where real people live their lives out. Of course, there has been no shortage
of attempts to subvert this distinction.

And yet the fact that it makes considerable sense in the mind means that one is more than simply able to understand it, to reject it or not at will, but that it has a certain call on us, that it is difficult to wriggle free from.

We can certainly imagine — at least imagine — a difference between media representation and what we might call "everyday life," which is sometimes "the represented." And once we imagine this difference, it lingers.

The realm of mass media can be thought of as something with effects on and that is received by or contradicted by the ground level, which is often conceived of as the level of ethnographic analysis. Discursive constructions carried in media of global, state, and/or cultural scope, perhaps forming national, gender, ethnic, or sexual identities or creating particular historicities and senses of place and time, can be seen to be formed within the special realm of film. Or such social facts can be seen to be symptomatically reflected in film. Either way. And then film emanates these powers of construction (or reproduction and reinforcement) to the ethnographic ground, a ground that might variously be formed by or perhaps alter or contest cinema's power to generate reality effects.

This is certainly a fruitful approach to media or film studies and a particularly strong one in cultural studies and anthropology: to analyze and debate, for instance, the role of cinema in constructing national identities. Or to analytically tie representations of gender and sex in film to nation or state projects of modernization or to colonial legacies. Or one can link the narrative flow of time in cinema to the structural transformations of capital and the like. This is, without doubt, a most productive field of scholarship, a field that results from the conception of film or media as having a distinct, transmittable power to shape and structure the life that happens in ethnographic reality. One can read it as symptom of the structure or causative agent in its formation, or both.

Now what I want to bring into contact with this distinction between representation and ground is a body of cinematic work that I think provides us with some unsettling dimensions with which to think this through differently: there are unsettling ways in which Asian horror cinema interacts with "ethnographic reality." But before getting into that, it might be helpful to consider the following scene . . .

‫⍺‬ *Nang Nak* (1997) was one of the first recent Thai films to achieve global recognition and audiences,[1] and this scene from the film might stand in for an important philosophical, if not theological, issue at play in any question about the relations between mass media and the "ground level" of ethnographic analysis.

The issue that I want to bring forward here concerns the idea of *two worlds*, a *this world* and a *world beyond*, existing sometimes in parallel and sometimes in crossing.

The scene takes place after a young man, Mak, has been drafted into military service, has a near-death experience, and returns home to his wife, Nak, and their child, both of whom, it turns out, have died during the birth and are actually now ghosts.

While villagers are horrified by the ghost Nak, who has been occasionally haunting them, and are now also creeped out by crazy Mak, who is living with her, a monk from a nearby temple visits Mak to try to convince him that he is not seeing reality but, in truth, is living in a world of illusions constructed by his dead wife.

Mak believes himself to be living with his wife and child in an ideal home. We see the couple eat and sleep together, have conversations and even sex, and love and care for their baby together. In the movie segments dominated by Nak's power to construct reality in her husband's mind, everything looks idyllic. But in reality-oriented vision, Mak is disheveled, living in a dilapidated house that he sees as clean and whole, and he speaks to empty air.

Others see his sorry state, knowing that his wife and child are, in fact, dead and that his reality has therefore been arrested by the spectral world of her ghost.

Is it possible that we can compare the relation of the plane of fictional, constructional media realities to the ground of the everyday as being somewhat like the power that holds sway over Mak and keeps him trapped in an alternate reality? Perhaps the media realm possesses only a less powerful and complete power over us than that of this exceptionally powerful ghost over Mak. And if so, then, the local monk's position — the invocation for Mak to wake up out of the dreamworld — would surely also be present in both cases, or really, we might speak of three cases here:

Come see for yourself.
Is he human or a ghost?

....

Seeing through the dream worlds that cinema constructs.

Waking up from spells cast by supernatural entities.

Reflexively self-checking the perceptual apparatus of anthropology: Is it too carried away by representationalism and *the idea of* the discursive constructive power of mass-mediated realities? And if it is, can it bring itself back to the "ground level"? Or better, where else can it bring itself?

Reality, the Medium

Does waking up out of media reality demand the mindfulness and concentration that the monk demands of Mak, to wake up out of the spells it casts? What relation can there really be between the second option above, "waking up from spells cast by supernatural entities," and the other items, which are set within a different world, a world that includes social science, a real world that operates on wholly separate principles?

Here, I am speaking of what is perhaps a new set of two worlds, the two worlds that are sometimes labeled as the world of "belief" and the world of "reality." And any exploration of this, it seems to me, would benefit from passing through Freud's discussion of the uncanny, if only because his essay is so focused on breaches of enlightenment realism, and his sensibility

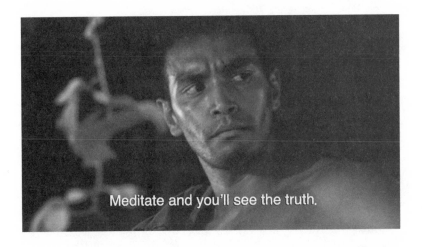

Meditate and you'll see the truth.

is, arguably, wound through the weft of realism that is commonly found in contemporary critical thinking, even if his specifically psychoanalytic symptomology is not. Not to mention the essay's obvious pertinence to the ghost world.

One of the great values of Freud's text today is that he is so willing to declare a commitment to a commonsense-scientific idea of reality, which in today's world of critical thought is not at all clearly admitted to with such direct honesty. And yet this confident faith is still present, very present, ever-present today. A lot of lip service is paid to the ideal of blurring the boundaries between reality and fiction or upsetting the foundational discourses of the European Enlightenment. But much of this lip service is arguably just distracting and empty noise, and one finds none of that in Freud. A spade is a spade, and we know perfectly well what we mean by reality here: the empirical, material world made up of things that really exist and that is apprehensible to both the everyday common empirical senses and to scientific observation and analysis. Freud's starting point provides us, then, with an honest starting point and also a position from which to begin to explore how or why it might be possible or desirable to unsettle our sense of the real, to doubt it, or finally even question that we know for sure what we are referring to when we speak in this way. And the way I propose that we can begin this questioning is to provisionally name it and then concentrate on and contemplate it in order to take a good look at it. Borrowing very loosely in form from Dipesh Chakrabarty's *Provincializing Europe*, we might call this "Reality1" (reminiscent of "History1").[2] Ironically, it will be my argument that the longer we look at Reality1, the more it starts to get really unstable. And this, I think, is something that greatly concerned Freud and was the impetus for his concept of the uncanny.

His essay is about the strange feeling, of being *creeped out*, the creeped-out uncanny that opens up when phenomena occur that should not be possible in Reality1. The modern, enlightened worldview has cast out primitive superstition, and yet . . .

And yet sometimes things are not what they seem. How can the breaches and tears in Reality1 — how can the uncanny — be brought back into the purview of the Reality1 principle? This is the big question for Freud, and he approaches it from two angles.

On the one hand is the world of fiction, which has ways of inculcating uncanny experiences in readers. On the other hand, we have, in real life itself, uncanny experiences that occur even if unbidden. Freud brings the uncanny in fiction and the uncanny in real life together into one analysis, and this seems absolutely crucial. He winds up defining each, fiction and real life, through the other.

But clarifying Reality1 may not be an obvious mission of Freud's, at least not on the manifest level. In fact, he almost obsessively goes immediately in the opposite direction, launching the essay with an elaborate attempt to establish a cross-cultural referent for the uncanny itself, going to several languages and doing an amateur etymological analysis of various words in various languages that he asserts are used to indicate this elusive but very real feeling. Here he recognizes, astutely, the inadequacy of any single word or language to capture this feeling, which in German is *das Unheimliche*. He misses, because there were no future travel or time machines available to him in those days, my usage, "creeped out." And yet he at least intuits that, as we will see here, it is precisely cultural and temporal shifts in the register of reality that the uncanny is about and that his linguistic analysis can somehow mirror and reflect.

Having passed through the extended attention to the concept of nonordinary reality embodied linguistically in words for the uncanny, Freud turns to fiction and ghost stories, though it soon becomes clear that Freud's concern becomes far more about defining the real world and the enlightened, rational, materialist view that knows it as such than it is about exploring fiction. For here Freud defines the uncanny in binary partnership with the assumed experience of minds that have *surmounted* superstitious and primitive beliefs. And this word, *Überwundensein* or *überwundene*, almost always appears italicized, is insisted upon over and over — we the modern have *surmounted* primitive superstitious beliefs but are nevertheless still vulnerable to relapse.

This slippage and misplacement, the momentary appearance of a feeling of reality to the supernatural rather than a feeling of reality confined only to Reality1, is what gives us this fleeting feeling of the uncanny.

"As soon as something actually happens in our lives which seems to support the old, discarded beliefs we get a feeling of the uncanny."[3]

We educated Europeans live in a disenchanted world, and it is precisely that fact that amplifies and defines the feeling of the uncanny, the unexpected contrast with that world that the apparent reality of spirits, demons, and such presents.

"Nowadays we no longer believe in them, we have *surmounted* such ways of thought; but we do not feel quite sure of our new set of beliefs, and the old ones still exist within us ready to seize upon any confirmation."[4]

Thoughts that were thought to be dead, passed, are, in fact, still present. We are, in effect, still haunted by undead thoughts, which still live on somewhere, in the recesses of the mind.

They are *within us* . . .

Waiting to seize us . . .

Are the thoughts threatening to *mount* us? Can these thoughts possess us? Reverse our surmounting of them?

Them. They came from within. The thoughts.

"And conversely, he who has completely and finally dispelled animistic beliefs in himself, will be insensible to this type of the uncanny. . . . For the whole matter is one of 'testing reality,' pure and simple, a question of the material reality of the phenomena."[5]

To be psychically invulnerable, living wholly within the reality principle, Reality1, is admirable indeed. Something Freud himself was not able to attain by his own implicit admissions of uncanny experiences but which, he seemed also to imply, is entirely possible and already the case for others, for the fully mature European man.

By contrast, uncanny experiences occur "when repressed infantile complexes have been revived by some impression, or when primitive beliefs we have surmounted seem once more to be confirmed."[6] As is well known, "savages" and "primitives" are, in standard European form, conceived as children whose thoughts reflect infantile neuroses. Freud insists that in considering our difference from primitives, we must "respect a perceptible psychological difference here, and to say that the animistic beliefs of civilized people have been *surmounted* — more or less."[7]

By contrast, the storyteller of fiction has a paradoxical relation to the uncanny. This because the "reality-testing" faculty is in abeyance.

"The story-teller has this license among many others, that he can select his world of representation so that it either coincides with the realities we are familiar with or departs from them in what particulars he pleases. We accept his ruling in every case."[8]

"In the realm of fiction many things are not uncanny which would be so if they happened in real life."[9]

And yet fiction, if framed in just the right way, can actually produce more uncanny effects than reality under certain conditions. The main condition being that the fictional frame must be one that reproduces as faithfully as possible the reality-principles of the real world.

Realism + ghost = more uncanny sensations.

"So long as they remain within their realm of poetic reality their usual attribute of uncanniness fails to attach to such beings."[10] This is the case once the reader accepts the frame that he is moving through a fantasy world. Ghosts might appear, but this is only expectable in the fantastic world constructed by the author.

"The situation is altered as soon as the writer pretends to move in the world of common reality."[11]

When fiction writers adopt the conventions of any kind of realism, or even more, simulate nonfiction, this is precisely the setup for producing uncanny feelings in the reader, the more so if the account pretends to actually be a true story. It is this type of ghost story, the one that attempts to be real, that is the greatest purveyor of the uncanny.

Freud's own ghost story is supremely realistic, for when we are being told the scientist's analysis of the uncanny, the frame is that *we are to understand the analysis as nonfictional.* Freud's story of the thoughts from a precivilized memory, haunting somewhere still in our minds, is the scary story being told in the essay. A true story. It must be emphasized, however, that Freud is not, ostensibly, telling a fictional story. That is why it is so uncanny! It is real, a truth in the frame of Reality1 that Freud is presenting in his essay, which is not, ostensibly, a work of fiction. And what appears in the real (even if it does not belong there) is, as he explains, the best purveyance of the creepy.

But there is a problem, according to Freud, when a storyteller feigns reality and has been playing with us all along: it leaves a psychic residue behind.

"He takes advantage, as it were, of our supposedly surmounted superstitiousness; he deceives us into thinking that he is giving us the sober truth, and then after all oversteps the bounds of probability. We react to his inventions as we should have reacted to real experiences; by the time we have seen through his trick it is already too late and the author has achieved his object."[12]

Revealing the trick, that what was described as real was in fact fiction, is, however, a cause of unrest: "We retain a feeling of dissatisfaction, a kind of grudge against the attempted deceit."[13]

And so there is also a distinction between something that is really uncanny and that which is not, a real uncanny and an unreal uncanny, the latter of which gives birth to a *grudge* . . .

Were we not in an educated European world, it would be dangerous for writers to traffic in this kind of fiction, as the effect of such thoughts, this grudge, might be harmful. If angers and grudges had effects that radiated out of the private psychic experiences of readers and circulated about in the world with a lingering power of their own, then it would not only be deceitful but also dangerous to traffic in this fiction.

(But, luckily, as Benjamin Whorf points out, for Standard Average European grammar, cause and effect stop at the container of the skull.[14] Thoughts, as events, happen only within the skull and do not have effects on anything outside of the skull.)

And so it is precisely this dangerous brinksmanship, which is not *really* dangerous, between reality and fiction that is the crucible in which uncanny sensations are forged in fiction and in even greater quantity than in reality, no doubt due to the fact that uncanny events are hard to come by in reality but are produced at the flick of a pen in fiction.

At every stage in Freud's story, the uncanny appears in order to clarify Reality1, attempting to precisely mark this pairing of borders: between reality and superstition on one hand and between reality and fiction on the other. And in so doing, both superstition and fiction, through their concurrent relation to reality, are brought into relation with each other. Not directly, mind you, but through the *medium* of Reality1.

But if Reality1 brings fiction and the supernatural into relation, serving as their medium, it is important to remember one thing about mediums: once they begin channeling, they are no longer the ones in control.

This is, then, in excess of a disparaging look at religious views or cultural Others. It is also, albeit not by intent, a wake-up call to the power of "reality" to create uncanny effects, of *"reality" to be the real source of terror*: Reality1's precise production of this inherent, unstable property of its own self. *Thus, wherever this kind of reality can be found, in ourselves, in others, there, too, will be found the possibility for something to creep out of it.* For Freud, what creep out from this kind of reality are the haunting thoughts, thoughts that will not stay dead, thoughts of a dark past of the European self but also of Others, of savage and primitive minds.

They are *within us* . . . waiting to seize us . . . thoughts threatening to *mount* us . . . possess us . . . reverse our surmounting of them . . . *them*. They came from within, the thoughts . . .

It is no wonder, then, that fiction of the supernatural that comes from sources foreign to the European, and from their misty realm of belief and religion, might have a double pull to anyone inducted into Reality1. In fact, Freud's emphasis was on the return of dead, old European ideas, not the entrance of foreign spirits. And yet foreign primitives and their thoughts represent for Freud a version of the European past, the surmounted, and so are equivalent in some formal sense with the underside of European thought, which threatens to seize the mature man.

And as for "foreign fictions," which Freud did not address in detail, might they have a double call on this sense of haunting, a power available to the author, because not only has one not conquered the haunting thoughts, not only has the story of Reality1 not reached its happy, invulnerable end, but might foreign stories of the uncanny summon these haunting thoughts and then compound that with a *fear that these thoughts will bind in legion with their allies on the outside*, with images called forth from an *Other* fiction or Other culture?

Thus, precisely on this turning point in the idea of the uncanny, of an assumption of a geo-cultural rootedness of the haunting thoughts from a past time and a belief that the European past lives on in a diffuse and generalized primitive present, the double-haunted potential flowers, a combinatorial possibility of identity of those thoughts with the foreign. Here the spirit medium of Reality1 brings the European and its Others, its doubles, into relation, into contact, and into a possible union.

Ghosts of the world . . .

Spirit Doubles

The lack of control, of a reality that has become a medium, that is serving as the conduit that brings fiction and the spirit world into contact with each other, a reality that in essence surrenders its autonomous self for the sake of bringing the parties into relation, is particularly uncanny when it comes to the relation between mediaworlds and ethnographicworlds in the genre of current Asian horror cinema. This horror has catapulted Asian cosmologies of the spirit world across cultural boundaries within Asia and, of course, across the Pacific as well, echoing further in Hollywood remakes. This cinema depends so much for its life — its simultaneous local, regional, and global reach — not only on the inclusion of ethnographic content and its translation across cultures but also on translations between the ground level of ethnographic reality and the world of media representation. And when I speak of translations between ethnographic reality and the world of media representation, I mean translation both ways: not merely the inclusion of ethnographic content within the realm of media representation but also the distinct appearance in ethnographic reality of entities emanating from this other media world.

Consider, for instance, the following fact about the local and international success of Japan's *Ringu*,[15] which was the biggest spark of the Asian horror cinema explosion of which *Nang Nak* was also part. At eleven AM on August 10, 2002, on the first day of the Japanese Hungry Ghost festival at LaForet Museum in Harajuku, a fashionable shopping district in Tokyo, a funeral ceremony was held for Yamamura Sadako, the ghost character of *Ringu*. The event was staged to symbolically put her troubled soul to rest and followed Buddhist ceremonial rituals for the dead. The character was fictional, first generated in popular novels. The author, Suzuki Koji, expressed his apologies to all women named Sadako for what he had done to their name.[16]

Arguably, the rise of this Asian cinema wave was driven by the inclusion of what we might call the "ethnographic realities" in these films, which contribute to both their regional and international appeals. Sadako, for instance, coincides with traditional Japanese visions of *yurei*, in this case the particular variant of the vengeful ghost manifesting as ghost due to the power of anger. Regionally, this form translates to other local Asian traditions while also carrying the sense of cultural difference, its Japanese cultural variation, along with it. It is perhaps less culturally familiar in the West, of course, and this incursion of foreign spirit form has been considered one important factor in the international appeal of so-called J-horror and Asian horror among audiences whose own horror traditions have been stretched to their limit of replayability.

Now this interplay between media and reality levels is particularly convoluted in the case of *Nang Nak* and is actually not *capped off by* a rite to her spirit *but begins with one*. The director of *Nang Nak*, Nonzee Nimbutr, had to appease Nang Nak herself, and for that, the first place he went was to the shrine that has been built up around her memory and has become a center for a cult to her spirit. The cult of Mae Nak (Mother Nak) has grown steadily throughout the last forty years of her mass-mediated representation. Mae Nak has been made into an estimated forty or more TV and film versions as well as into stage plays and even a classical-style opera. Every version is a commercial success with Thai audiences, who never seem to tire of it.

The story of Nang Nak, or Mae Nak as she is most commonly called, is actually an old legend in Thailand and is the most common ghost story in the country, the master ghost story that defines the others. Nak is a particularly dangerous and powerful form of spirit, of a woman who has died in childbirth. Her love for her husband brings her back in an unstable form of unnatural family life. He must wake up to that fact, and when he does, Nak's ghost becomes consumed with attachment and must eventually be put to rest by monks while Mak hides out in a temple.

The shrine to Mae Nak, or Mother Nak, is on the grounds of Wat Mahabutr in Prakanong, Bangkok, the temple where Mak is said to have hidden out. Before filming, Nonzee brought the main cast and crew to the shrine, where they made traditional offerings of flowers, fruit, candles, incense, money, bananas, and a pig's head to her spirit; asked her permission to make the film; and asked for her mercy and forgiveness should they make any misstep (and I have asked the same of her myself). Nonzee then toured the rest of the country, making offerings at famous shrines to spirits to seek the spiritual backing and ghostly green light for his film. Note that quite unlike Sadako and her funerary rites, however, Nang Nak and her spirit cult already specifically existed in a cultural, legendary pantheon while, in fact, owing her prominence in part to the mediaworld that had cultivated her presence and grown her cult into its present state.

Generally, and although there is no hard historical evidence that she ever existed, Mae Nak is considered to have lived and died in childbirth sometime during the reigns of either Kings Rama III, IV, or V, variously sometime between 1851 and 1910. The story takes place in the Prakanong district, which is now part of metropolitan Bangkok but was once a rural Thai village crisscrossed by streams and canals. Mae Nak is said to have haunted her husband and chased him into Wat Mahabutr Temple, where he took refuge and where Mae Nak was finally put to rest. She is now believed to have been buried under a tree in the temple. That is where her spirit house has arisen, next to the twelve-foot-tall stump of the Takien tree, which remains on the grounds. People flock to the tree stump to rub its surface with blessed oil and their hands in search of impressions that can be interpreted as the shape of lottery numbers. Its surface is worn down, oily smooth. Offerings are placed at the foot of this tree while adjacent is an elaborate shrine to Mae Nak, her "home," where her statue and that of her baby await a steady flow of worshippers, particularly on prelottery runup time. For donations of ten or twenty baht (twenty-five or fifty cents) one can get either the standard prepared suit of offerings, including sweet incense, a candle, a flower garland, and a small bit of gold leaf to affix to her statue, or the special version, which includes an orchid and bottle of fragrance. More dedicated followers prepare their offerings at home and include candy, fruit, wreaths, and sometimes also a pig's head. Others bring hordes of makeup, lipstick, beauty soap, and shampoo as well as balls, toys, diapers, milk, and formula for her baby. The shrine room is overflowing with these gifts, which have to be regularly switched out. The walls are lined with paintings of Mae Nak in various styles interspersed with the finest embroidered silk dresses to be seen anywhere, all brought as gifts to her. Her statue, and that of her baby in her arms, is covered in layers of gold leaf, which has been lovingly affixed to her form by followers.

Surrounding the shrine are scores of fortune tellers, seers, psychics, and lottery sellers who tap into the resonance that Mae Nak's spirit generates in the realms of fortune and supernatural intervention.

The followers, from all classes, ages, genders, and professions, come seeking her aid in difficult life matters and seek her protective blessings. She is also especially reputed to help with lottery numbers. The largest portion of followers are young women who come to her with issues of love, marriage, and economic security. There are also many young men who will soon enter the military draft lottery (draw a black ball and you are free, a red ball and you are conscripted). Since she hates the draft, which took her husband away, she is predisposed to help the odds be ever in your favor.

Of course, as mentioned before, there are also now the visits from filmmakers seeking to bring Mae Nak's spirit again to the screen. No doubt she also has a vested interest in these undertakings as they broadcast and sustain her cult. The most recent visit has come from a British production team, who made a remake of the Thai classic for contemporary times. And this is a peculiar mutation in World Gothic. The British writer and director penned a tale of a couple in urban Prakanong, Bangkok, named Nak and Mak, who become haunted by Mae Nak's ghost. Written by a Brit with little experience with the country and no knowledge of Thai language, the film was, in fact, a Thai-language feature, made with simultaneous local and global aspirations like the international feature *Nang Nak*, which was written and directed by Thais. *The Ghost of Mae Nak* was a minor hit in Thailand and made it to number three in the box office (compared to the number one of Nonzee's version, which beat out *Titanic* at the time).[17] However, in the West, the British-Thai *Ghost of Mae Nak* had little festival play and almost no theatrical release and was an international failure for reasons probably having to do with the fact that the film is what I can only describe as deeply sucky.

Despite its lack of interest as either art or entertainment in the West, what is interesting anthropologically about this British remake of a Thai Gothic horror story, written in English and translated into a Thai script and then played back for Thai audiences, is how it inverts the relation present in *Ringu* between funeral offering, cinematic rendition, and cultural translation. As the wheels of production of the English-language, Hollywood version of *Ringu* rolled out as *The Ring*, and a new version of the yurei spirit was to appear in US shopping malls, now bearing the name of "Samara," Koji Suzuki, author of *Ringu*, said at the Tokyo funeral rite to Sadako, "Sadako's physical body has died. Her spirit has crossed the oceans, where it was reborn as Samara."

In one sense, this is the kind of ending that *Ringu* avoided, where a spirit is appeased and allowed to achieve its final passage to the afterworld. But perhaps the statement includes the logic of the film as well. Sadaku's curse landed on you if you did not pass the video on to others. If the funeral for this fictitious character settles Sadako's matters in Japan, Samara, the copy, has gone on to the next audience and the next screening, perhaps embodying the logic of the video curse in the story, protecting the Japanese audience, and passing the curse on to the Americans.

By contrast, the British remake of Mae Nak was explicitly conceived by its director/writer as a way to return her soul to final rest. Most versions of Mae Nak either have her spirit trapped in a vase in the river or, as in the 1997 version, has her powerful spirit condensed into a piece of bone taken from her skull, which is then used by a Monk as a powerful charm but is then lost in the ages. In the British remake, the characters eventually find the missing piece of bone, then find her buried skeleton, and return the bone to its place in the hole in her skull and so put the spirit finally to rest.

Thus, the curse is bounced back into, and buried in, Asia, from whence it came.

The cast and crew of the British version also made the pilgrimage to the shrine of Mae Nak to receive her blessing and support for the film, adhering strictly to the protocols for propitiating the spirit of Mae Nak. The filming was reported to go off without the usual number of hitches and problems accompanying something as complex as film production.

And this returns us to these questions of ghosts, media, and ethnographic levels of reality to which, in turn, one more dimension can be

Nak. Ghosts must be with ghosts.

added in this series of correspondences. I have left it for last to mention that at the shrine to Mae Nak, off at a slight angle to the side but definitely within view of the statue's line of sight, is placed a TV set that is always left on, twenty-four hours a day, for Mae Nak to watch. Mostly soap operas.

This votive television set plays media constructions to a spirit in a shrine partly supported by media constructions and, in fact, on occasion plays back for her spirit media representations of her own story so that the spirit can watch herself on mortal TV.

What epistemological operation can ethnographic analysis use to pry open and find the ground here, keeping in mind that sometimes there are also film crews, directors, and writers on the scene as well, making offerings to the spirit who is watching herself on TV before they make new representations of her that will play for her on TV, which are shaped in turn by their relationship with her cult and shrine, within this scene?

Is the impulse to be in the position of the monk to Mak, the position of occupying the ground of the real and possessing the clear sight to bring others out of their funk, somehow inadequate here? Or does this "scene" also show how inadequate the argument for constructive powers of media is as well?

Is there still a call, perhaps uncanny and a bit mysterious, coming from this other world — a spirit world or media world — that resists the insistence asked of it, that it show itself for what it plainly is and is not, the insistence that our perception of this realm can ever be returned back to the earth?

Ghosts of the world, unite!

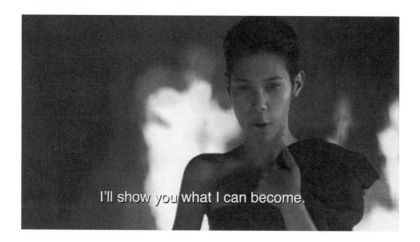

I'll show you what I can become.

3 · BETTING ON THE REAL

NOT LONG AGO, THE UNITED STATES INVADED IRAQ, and a tsunami hit the coast of Thailand, and before that there was the devastating financial crash of 1997. By December 2004 severe treatment of Muslim minorities in the South of Thailand had been ramping up, and small local networks of Muslim utopianists in the southern region of Thailand had been growing more violent, fueling the desire on all sides to make a clear and violent statement. Prime Minister Thaksin Shinawatra had cultivated his relationship with President George W. Bush and had been taking in secret rendition captives from the CIA for torture. Meanwhile, violence had become an entrenched part of life in the kingdom: the killing of government officials and schoolteachers in the largely Muslim south, bombings in the capital of Bangkok almost certainly planted by elite factions vying for an excuse to impose stability (a tried-and-true tactic of those seeking power), sweeping harassment and arrests of Muslims, and army and police violence. Economic, natural, and political disasters follow one after another, not fast enough that each failed to leave its own unique imprint but fast enough for the dead to crowd in, to press in on the living with increasingly urgency, and backed up by an inability of the cognito-cultural infrastructure to process so many spirits so fast. Unlike in social science, in real life there is no patrol to enforce the barrier between the living and the dead, no way to keep all of them out, and there are far too many around to expel.

Foreign ghosts are a big problem. The ghosts of tourists who died on the island beaches are among the most problematic, since they do not have relatives around and are so far from home, cut off by the tsunami. Stories run wild of foreigners haunting taxicabs and hotels or running aimlessly on the beach. Uncountable rituals are staged all over the shorelines, including one in which ninety-nine monks were brought to the beach (double nines) to comfort the unrest. And yet, several years later, even after live foreign tourists have returned (but not the Thai or Chinese tourists), there are still ghosts with aching hearts pressing in on the coasts of the kingdom. Stories of this still pass freely among both locals and the visitors, creating a new subtext of information in beach tourism, which is as common, though less traceable, as the published travel guides of our lonely planet.

After the world-currency-gambling and neoliberal investment schemes in the late 1990s erupted into the Asian currency crisis, and the Thai national money suddenly plummeted in value, and everything of value that was denominated in Thai numbers was halved in a matter of days; now, when the national identity and national economy as nominally defined have suddenly been revealed to be empty, when this enormous catastrophe in the accumulation and interpretation of value in the marks and records of memories of trades in marks and records has made its impact on the physical existence and subsistence of practically everyone in the country . . . gambling explodes everywhere. The Thai national lottery has to expand the issue of tickets several times, the black-market lottery grows tremendously, and full-blown casinos spring up as a border industry in Burma and Cambodia. People begin flocking over the borders to gamble where it is legal, and soon a national campaign is launched to keep people and their Thai money within the geographical border of the nation. Money is, they claim, being drained out across the border precisely at a time when currency reserve is such an important issue and problem. Every road out of the kingdom is peppered with signs exhorting Thais to go back, to turn back, to be patriotic about their money, to not weaken the nation. The closer you get to the border, the more signs there are, taking an increasingly urgent moral tone, declaiming the evils of gambling and threatening hell for the gambler in the next world. Here, as on the coasts, the border has to be shored up and the flow and exchange of immaterial entities dampened down.

The nation pulsates with ghosts and numbers, unrestful spirits and flighty monies, pushing in and out on the borders of the nation, which, paradoxically, become less and less about geographic and material space and more about a seemingly abstract and immaterial existence to the nation, which nevertheless alights upon those material borders, transposing on them a different register of form and meaning.

What is this existence, this new national entity and principle of form, which communicates itself in a cosmos or global situation that is also, suspiciously, digitized and perhaps immaterial? Is this Deleuze and Guattari's deterritorialization or Hardt and Negri's ether?[1] The realm of the spirits and ghosts and the ethereal — a commonplace, commonsensical linguistic habit of reference to the new global electronic media and infocom forms, and a kind of sci-fi-like theory, such as its appearance in *Empire*. It may be noticed that in this flight into spiritual tropoi to understand deterritorialization, there is no place for real ghosts; they are only metaphor. This tropological spectralism is intended to be taken seriously: the ether can function as the master concept of Empire and as the global communication medium in a sci-fi-like tome about its unique deterritorializing capacities: "Communication is not satisfied by limiting or weakening modern territorial sovereignty; rather it attacks the very possibility of linking an order to space."[2] And what if it did attack this possibility? This is precisely the kind of question science fiction asks: to ask "what if?" and proceed to tell a story from there. What if it became impossible to link the global order to space? In contrast to "what if," social science says, as we know, "this is so." While science fiction may say literally the same words, "this is so," what it really means is "what if this is so?" Social science likes to make its statements far less equivocal.

And then what sort of existence would we all have now, now that we all must commune in some way with this ether?

"Here we reach an extreme limit of the process of the dissolution of the relationship between order and space. At this point we cannot conceive of this relationship except in *another space*, an elsewhere that cannot in principle be contained in the articulation of sovereign acts."[3]

The ether.

ether?

All sovereignty, Hardt and Negri proclaim, "dissolves in the ether."[4] Every bodily and material manifestation of space is reordered by the ether into something wholly other. In the epic story of Empire, the ether is the master trope of the new Empire, which properly speaking has three facets: the bomb, money, and the one that completes and surpasses the others, the ether. All three share the characteristic of exerting a deterritorializing force. The bomb represents the continuous state of generalized death that hangs over the global situation, the "'non-place' of life, or, in other words, as the absolute capacity for destruction."[5] Money, similarly, loses much of its specific, place-based power of sovereignty, which then becomes bound to a network of global centers: "As national monetary structures tend to lose any characteristics of sovereignty, we can see emerging through them the shadows of a new unilateral monetary reterritorialization that is concentrated at the political and financial centers of Empire, the global cities."[6] But the ultimate force is the ether, which differs from the other two because all "residues" of the spatial order are lost in it:

> The space of communication is completely deterritorialized. It is absolutely other with respect to the residual spaces that we have been analyzing in terms of the monopoly of physical force and the definition of monetary measure. Here is a question not of residue but of metamorphosis: a metamorphosis of all the elements of political economy and state theory. Communication is the form of capitalist production in which capital has succeeded in submitting society entirely and globally to its regime, suppressing all alternative paths.[7]

This is, of course, an attempted extension of Deleuze and Guattari's concept of deterritorialization,[8] which even more than social scientific concepts does not always behave predictably. So let us go further. For deterritorialization is something essential to the adaptability of territories and for their establishment, their order and norm and control. But it is also a principle of freedom and possibility and, in any case, somewhat akin to the states of things as they are emerging and becoming. In the case of the story of Empire, the deterritorialization of the ether is the leading edge of capitalism's current deterritorializations. Just as the establishment of labor power and the regime of the wage once deterritorialized the body, person, and product of work in their prior arrangement, it instigated the reterritorialization of the body, person, and product in a system of labor power and commodities. This process played itself out in actual space, in the disenfranchisement of farmers and their migration from rural lands and their reterritorialization into factories and cities.

But this deterritorialization-reterritorialization, as well as that enacted by the ether, can in Deleuzian terms be said to be "relative" deterritorialization occurring on the molar level, the level of social science proper, the level of gross matter, the apparent level of mass and structure (states, classes, and organizations of factory capital and even financial capital as well as the plane on which it makes sense to say there are such things as individuals and societies), where bodies seem to collide with other bodies, exerting power and influence in a mechanical physics of matter and power. There is, however, another kind of deterritorialization, "absolute," which is represented by philosophy (of course) and by molecular processes that are ontologically prior to the apparent world and are politically and morally more valued in Deleuze and Guattari for the suggestion that they contain within them unanticipated possibilities for life that escape, every day and right here and now, the operations of what we might call "power" in other kinds of political philosophy, which normally refers only to the molar level. The world is, in fact, seething with these molecular processes, many of which are taking lines of flight beyond our notice, consistent only in their variance and flight. In that sense, deterritorialization cannot be said, in general, to be entirely a negative process — that is,

"We are being uprooted."

"Our natural relation to our senses is being violently abstracted."

"People now no longer feel connected to each other."

"I don't know who or what I am anymore."

"The product of our labor is no longer a material object."

"I am no longer sure what is solid and real about my body anymore."

"Money is no longer grounded in gold, or the real economy, where it should be, but is completely fictitious, abstract . . ."

"Or, ghostly."

"I am losing my mind," etc.

— nor can deterritorialization be said to be liberating only, for obviously its operation is essential to the development of molar structures of domination in general and the operation of the capitalist machine in particular. And what is more, and this is rare for viral French philosophies, there is a very clear discourse in Deleuze and Guattari regarding the dangers of deterritorializing one's life: it can be "horribly botched." There is always a possible catastrophe in constructing, or contacting (the distinction is deliberately not clear in Deleuze and Guattari), a so-called Body without Organs, or BwO, their construction from Antonin Artaud of a plane of bodily existence that completely eschews the body of a discrete organism operating according to an internal harmony of parts and instead reaches into a broader plane of permeability and copresence with other bodies as well as forces that are, at least from the standpoint of convention, chaotic and absorbed and passed between bodies by osmotic processes. Deleuze and Guattari both celebrate this in a stereotypical avant-garde manner, and yet in a rarer form, issue warnings about caution, patience, and slow, deliberate exploration of the openings and becomings rendered possible by this absolute deterritorialization — Artaud's agonized life and Guattari's clinical experience with schizophrenics providing some guidance, no doubt.

On a very broad level, as well, there are dangers to deterritorializing processes, including, of course, the ethereal process of deterritorialization that is crucially linked to the massive molar story of Empire, certainly at least within that story's imagined world. And within the sci-fi-like story of Empire, such deterritorialization actually seems to have an almost absolute sense about it in that the ether is almost of another plane than either the bomb or money and was said to be "absolutely other." In a twist on Deleuze and Guattari's terms, we might almost want to call it an absolute relative deterritorialization: on the plane of relative deterritorialization, it has an absolute presence (in the story of Empire).

Of course, we might prefer a more realistic social science.

But should we? Should we assess concepts by their ability to create a semblance of that which they represent, the classic epistemic order of representational truth? Or do we instead assess them according to a political aesthetic, for instance whether this tale of Empire collapses differences and identities, such as race, class, and gender, and is therefore politically unacceptable? And in any case, is there something too utopian in its proposed alternative, an interconnected multitude of multiplicities?

Under the regime of realist verisimilitude, or that of positioning on a politico-aesthetic grid,[9] or even seen from a practically minded sensibility about what is possible and realistic to hope for from the world (although note that the book did lend inspiration to political action, which is rare), this story of Empire may not hold up. But perhaps the value of the heuristic of the ether in Empire might best be appreciated as speculative rather than realist (despite the fact that realism appears to be the vein and stylistics in which it is intended). Looked at from the scope of realistic social science, the story of Empire, of course, is not even nearly true in those terms. But might the presence of speculative fictions, science fictions here, allow us to see something with a clarity we might not have otherwise? The point not being Is this really what is happening? but rather, when we think this way, What do we — or do we not — see? Or even more radically Deleuze-Guattarian, What becomes actual as a result?

And yet, although I am recommending this to you, it is a bit hypocritical of me because I also have some serious concerns right here and now. The more I look into these memories from Deleuze and Guattari and their proliferation of terms, the more they seem to stick, to live on, beckoning me. I cannot seem to get them out of my system. I am not sure what is going on here, because I was able to take and immediately drop any idea from scholarly study, but these are strangely harder to drop. These almost chaotic words emanate like radiation out of my memories of texts a strange, resilient life that infiltrates my mind. I have no intent or desire to reproduce, apply, have fidelity to, or be accurate about Deleuze and Guattari. Quite the opposite: I want to rid myself of it. But when I try to take hold of these ideas to cast them out, I cannot find what it is exactly that I can hold on to, to grasp, shove, or strike out at.

I would think twice, if I were you, about reading further, because in here there might be submolar radiation effects. This will probably not be your first exposure, of course. But how many more times can you be exposed to this before it is too late? Who among us knows? And how do you know that accepted safety levels will not be revised at a later date?

Of course, much hard sci-fi proceeds with the containment-genre barrier of the premise that the supernatural is simply what a being perceives when he cannot understand the material that really matters. Or, as has been famously said in Arthur C. Clarke's third law of prophesy, "Any sufficiently advanced technology is indistinguishable from magic."[10] And *Em-*

pire as science fiction, and the communications ether that is its tropological "supernatural," retains that barrier as does most social science. That is what is so confounding when it comes to contemplating money, numbers, mathematics, geometry, and other abstract entities that have their origins in a less contained world. What might a sci-fi (or anthropology or social science) of money miss when founded on the premise that everything arises from a substance called matter, a substance that is beyond doubt as to whether it actually exists?

And yet even taking *Empire* just as a sci-fi historical fiction with a singular epic story, it makes one wonder whether life is, in fact, like this now even as it occurs within social science's genre parameters: increasingly constituted in the most fundamental sense by something that is the epitome not of the "concrete" but of the abstract — digital communication — conducted in numbers that are often imagined precisely not as the qualitative aspects or attributes of things but are instead that which attempts to transcend such things so that they are no longer particular but equivalent to others in an abstract group or series. In everything from the operations of global finance to media to the minutiae of everyday life, such forms of digital representation and communication seem to become seriously influential and so become a fundamental constituting ground of existence. As "ground," these forms seem to be conceivable as material structure with less certainty than the other grounds in which social theory has founded its reality principle traditionally.

But . . . of course, we can always try to pin down the wires and tracks of the network, the routes of transmission, and other material structures that embody this ethereal existence and name *those* the reality, name those the truly crucial things, name those as the matter in which all these abstractions are housed, name those as the ground.

Thank goodness for the ground. It is so grounding.

The Spiritual Network

I have known Little Prince Wirachai, who phones it in to the Nextworld, since the Little Prince was a five-year-old boy. Funny thing is, he still is a five-year old boy almost fifteen years later.

To get your bearings, know that at this point it is 2004, and Little Prince has not changed, but his phone has. In the old days, Little Prince used a massive block of a toy mobile phone, the kind that has to be plugged back into its almost car-size battery (plastic), to keep a charge and connect up to the network. In this case, however, it was connected with a spiritual network where a powerful grandfather spirit would dispense crucial information by ethereal voice down through the toy mobile phone and through Little Prince and onto the alternatively desperate or bemused villagers who crowded him on most days. That was back then. Times change. Over the years, the toy phone has shrunk, little by little, with the advance of technology until it folds smartly in the palm of his hand, or the hand of his possession body depending on how you look at it. It flips open, but there is no touch screen — that should work to place the moment.

Before, black-market lottery dealers would crowd around there, in the waiting space outside the spirit hall where Little Prince Wirachai would appear. Now they cannot show themselves in public, the lottery dealers. Two months ago, the police swept the whole village looking for drug dealers on their list. The order came right from the top, from the prime minister in Bangkok. A three-month war on drugs that would rid the country once and for all from the scourge of meth, the rapid proliferation of speed that launched itself after the financial crash.

The ones they were looking for kept turning up dead, a bullet in the head. The villagers say the police offed them. The police say the mafia did it for fear of the police catching them and letting their tongues loose first. Amnesty International said there were three thousand people killed in three months. Those who dare not break the ban on black-market lottery for fear of the police weigh in on the matter through their lack of presence.

Now just the talk is left over, and that is more than enough to drive all the bet takers away from the courtyard outside the spirit house. No one wants to cross the law now. There is also a new law for everyone on motorbikes to wear safety helmets; but for that, people go on in their usual lawless and free-spirited way. Everyone just seems to know which laws are real — very real — and which are not.

People complain that their father or son or daughter did not deal or take drugs, and why did they have to be shot? But these deaths — far more common among the peoples and tribes that live in the hills than among those who live down here in the plains and foothills and are more thoroughly imagined as Thai — these deaths do not attract crowds, do not pull in more voices. It is not that anyone has any doubt that some of those three thousand who were executed without trial had to have been innocent. They are gamblers, and they know about numbers and odds. Some had to have been innocent; those are just the odds of it. The questions were really about the list, the list . . . who would be next on the list?

This is a time of reform, of change. After the crash, the meth spread faster than AIDS. Its name changed, too, with considerable promotion from the Interior Ministry, from *ya ma* ("horse drugs," which carried the connotation of strength for work) to *ya ba* ("crazy drugs"). After the crash, meth was, along with gambling, one of the only growth industries, and it took off in a vicious boom cycle that seemed, before the violence, to know no bust. Some of my host's friends from Northern Thailand have tried it out. They worked hard for years gathering mushrooms in the forest for some casual money for cigarettes and other fun things, but later, after the crash, when wild mushrooms became their only source of income . . . "We could work all day long without fail. You feel great, your body just keeps going and going and going."

But now, with such a fright about meth — a fright that has now seeped like the bloodstains into the realm of gambling, forcing the numbers takers into hiding and subtracting more than just a bit from the atmosphere surrounding Little Prince Wirachai on his toy cell phone network to the spiritual beyond — where is the superhuman strength to earn a living to come from? Not that such things as meth and black-market gambling are driven by necessity. They are consummate pleasures. Or is that a rather corrupt and rotten thing to say?

The sense of rot has been very efficiently communicated, transferred, routed around not only this local pocket of impact of the financial crash but all around a global network of values quite thoroughly connected to this whole situation. The wake of the financial crash in Thailand was not unlike that of 9/11 in the United States in how constrained all political discourse became. For many years, every issue and every debate had to pass through the dominating notion of "the economy" in Thailand. And since what was economic had gone all awry, reformation was the order of the day in every way. And that was true, of course, not only within Thailand but all across the globe in the moral pronouncements on Asian economies being distributed in abundance. In the wake of Enron's fall and all the other corporate accounting and investment banking scandals in the

United States at the turn of the century — and which did not seem to register any warning signals about the thoroughly corrupt money schemes that would appear later in the fall of 2008 — it may seem almost surprising to remember that only a few years before all that surfaced, after the 1997 crash of the Thai baht, the United States and other major global powers were vehemently focused on what they identified as the corruption endemic to Asian economies, far eastern places where something was rotten in the heart of globalization. Following the crash of the Thai baht in 1997, the economies that were identified as infected with "Asian contagion" and "Asian crony capitalism" were, for the most part, subjected to devastating consequences, including a rapid flight of investment and the requirement to submit to economically disastrous, ill-conceived, and high-handed "cures" from international governing organizations such as the IMF (International Monetary Fund).

The moral charges in such global power plays settled in and redistributed themselves in certain locations within the original offending place of the Asian crisis, Thailand. Quite famously in the late '90s, Asian economies, after the crash of the Thai baht, were portrayed in international discourse as dark, illegible cultural peculiarities. These discourses of othering occur internally as well, within Thailand, handed down toward certain internal populations within the country. Gamblers, spirit mediums, and informal money lenders, all of whom participate in complex economies of moral and monetary value, have since the postcrashing become a great concern of national attention and reform in Thailand. It is small-time (and often rural) practices of loaning and borrowing, of monetary speculation, and of supernatural forecasting that have become a focus of disciplinary attention and action in Thailand at the very same time that more legitimized forms of credit — specifically credit cards issued by banks with extensive global connections — have been expanding their reach.

Of course, establishing a causal, or conspiratorial, connection between the ascendance of one form of credit and the discrediting of other forms or even documenting this occurrence is not the point here. But just taking note of the simultaneity, one might think that critical anthropology would be well equipped to interpret the meaning of such coincidences, but it is difficult not to inadvertently mirror the moral mood and backdrop in which they are taking place. Global theoretical schemas that attempt to diagnose what is wildly wrong with globalization through attention to its effects on local peoples may trade in similar terms of othering in which the moral violations of globalization are highlighted by showing how those violations wind up causing culturally bizarre, reactive, and superstitious practices in local populations.[11] This is a problematic approach, given how it mirrors the wider fields of trade in global moralities, where the impulse to sort out the rational from the irrational and the comprehensible from the incomprehensible is often also tied to the project of sorting out the proper from the improper and even the allowed from the unallowed. In Thailand, seemingly "irrational," "superstitious," and "corrupt" practices of money have existed in ambiguous, contradictory relationships with complexes of moral value, a situation that has, until recently, been tolerated and considered tolerable in Thailand.

"Dark Finance"

In the Lampang Valley of Northern Thailand and under the sovereign sign of a Thai Buddhist money tree, the spirit of a young boy possesses a woman, and village people and others from farther locales hang on the child's words. All present must make presents of money, candy, and toys to the boy spirit, but they also place bills on twine sticks and attach them like leaves on the pole of the money tree. That is money earmarked for Buddhist dana, which is charitable giving to monks. On the day set aside for giving, the medium, in possession of herself, will lead a drunken parade of her village clients through the streets and into the temple, where the trees of money will be given over to the Buddhist monks, and then on to a committee that will build a new building for the village's governmental school.

Analogically, it is precisely the opposite of our maxim, "money doesn't grow on trees." Ours is an adage about the ontology of value in hard labor, a moral injunction to refrain from useless expenditure, and an ode to the economic real. But here in the shrine room of the boy spirit, people have come specifically in search of easy money. It is aftermath time in the Asian crisis, the Thai baht has crashed, and the bimonthly state lottery numbers are due out in a day, and that means a lot of hurting visitors for the young boy, who can give them a scoop on the numbers. For that insider information, they will pay the spirit a fee while at the same time a surplus is always expended to the Buddhist order through the blossoming money tree. The winning numbers are decided by the state's random drawing, but most bets will be placed on the last two or three numbers at modest odds in a diffuse, illegal black-market lottery in which the bet takers comprise anyone who is willing to promise a payoff according to competitively offered stakes and who can pay off the police or otherwise elude detection.

A lot of people have turned out for the possession session. On a toy cellular telephone, the boy spirit dials up and connects by network with bigger spirits in the world beyond, finding answers to his visitors' daily, mundane life problems. On the other end of the cell phone network, a "grandfather" spirit (Luang Bu) speaks from an elsewhere, to which the normal constraints of time and place no longer apply. He is hooked up from the beyond by wireless communication to those in the material world. But his first question about you, the first thing he must know before he can disclose anything to you, is your exact street and address number. Once your positioning in the grid of material space is established, he can then provide answers about your future and past.

When it comes to handing out the lottery numbers, it is the boy spirit down here on earth who is the source, passing out little tickets of numbers, which he writes each time for each guest, in exchange for gifts of cash, candy, and toys. As he bounces around to his favorite rock tunes played on an impressive stereo, the boy's arm rattles with gold bracelets, all presents of gold given to him by villagers after success with using his numbers.

I would have had to give him a gold bracelet myself if I had played the numbers that he gave away to me (for free). But unfortunately, lacking confidence, I did not buy a ticket. Instead, I took the little folded piece of paper with the child spirit's numbers written on it — which one is not supposed to disclose to anyone — and gave it to an avid numbers player in the area. She was going to play them, but she suddenly, inexplicably, changed her mind at the last minute. This, the child spirit's clients later explained, was because the numbers were meant for me, not her. That was why no one was able to place a bet on those numbers, which would have turned a 500-to-1 profit.

Locally, the reputation of this particular boy spirit for predicting the lottery has grown in leaps and bounds. How much he is making for his medium, one cannot know, but you can still do some accounting of his business by looking at the size of the money tree on display in the possession altar. It is full of bills, even big, lavish bills, an organically growing surplus for giving over to Buddhism. Here, in this trade of numbers, surplus value grows in leaps and bounds. This money is assembled and cultivated awaiting the first day of Buddhist Lent, a period of special renunciation for monks. The medium and her clients, after a daylong session of excessive drinking and dancing, will give all this money away in one sudden, great, blurry expenditure of pleasure and generosity. Around here, gambling under the sign of the money tree is practically the only symbolic context in which value can reproduce itself. Capital has dried up. Loans are hard to come by. And actual money in your hand is only worth half of what it was yesterday, unless you have dollars, which no one does. Everyone is going to have to change their plans, their habits, their expectations, their ideas. When seen through the lens of economy, so much about value and about the very nature of the progress and passage of time, in fact about the nature of being Thai and Asian, has changed so quickly, and this epistemological movement is no less shifty on the global order of things.

As one American investment manager put it at a conference, "Before the crash, the required book titles on every broker's shelf were *Asia Rising*; *The New Rich in Asia*; *The New Asian Renaissance*; *Asia's New World Order*; and *Thailand's Turn*. Now its *Asia Falling*; *Dragons in Distress*; *Manias, Panics, and Crashes*; *All the Trouble in the World*; *Japan Anything but Number One*; *Anatomy of a Bubble*; and *Tigers on the Brink*."[12] At one time the word "miracle" was almost a required prefix to any reference to Asian economies (up through 1996 and halfway through 1997 to be exact). Then it appeared to be different.

The discourses surrounding economic development in Asia in those years were heirs to a legacy. The image of the "Asian miracle economy" is an overdetermined figure of international orientalist discourse inscribing a complex of finely tuned values. As literary figure, it contains not only the despotic organization of an ant-like and ruthless capitalism with corresponding disciplined society but also dens of seething and free-wheeling greed. Asians are considered cheap and docile labor, but at the same time, nevertheless, energetic and industrious. They are said to continue ancestrally held hoarding practices of family saving but are also easily impressionable consumers. Discipline and excess, tight rule and capitalist abandon, these potent combinations of orientalist tropes were used to justify investment decisions of the West as often as they were used in Asia itself to define the political mandate of strong state rule and what seemed like a special cultural mixture of the market with nonmarket social and political relations. Possibly these were even superior forms of generating economic might. Right up to the last minute before the crash of the Thai baht in '97, the world was bullish on the Tigers and Dragons, backed strongly by the high returns on investment to the region. The World Bank and IMF continued their support of the "Asian way" to development, direct foreign investments were still flowing into Asia, Western banks continued to roll over short-term loans in foreign-denominated accounts, and Western investment firms were thoroughly exposed in many equity markets in Asia.

But there were surprises. With a slowdown in export growth for Thailand in '96 and '97, and after the highly liberalized international loan climate for the New World Economy throughout the '90s as advocated by the IMF and other international business interests, and with liberal availability of lending within Thailand, there was a generous flow of both Western and Japanese loans into the country, all of which propelled an extensive network of domestic business loans. With the growth that such loans afforded, expectations of returns rose, causing a feedback loop whereby it became "rational" to invest before costs would rise later. Investment in Thailand steadily increased, unabated. Thai business was heavily indebted to foreign capital interests in foreign-denominated accounts, which, however, no Western banks were reluctant to continue extending to the Thai miracle economy. The IMF was celebrating its global vision of freely flowing monetary exchange and issued a review of Thailand's economic fundamentals, which gave it, as well as many of its neighbors, a clean bill of health, echoing the majority of economists and financiers. While there are some criticisms written into IMF reviews (Why? More on this later . . .), no one disputes the fact that there was a continuous mood of general optimism around Asia.[13]

But July 1997 marked the end of the so-called miracle growth in the Asian economies, when the Bank of Thailand relented after months of attempting to defend the Thai baht's fixed exchange rate against speculators, a depleting foreign currency reserve, and mounting foreign-denominated debts in the private sector. Not surprisingly, the orientalist discourses of international finance suddenly transmuted as economists set the focus on what they called Asian "go-go capitalism," "cronyism," and "crony capitalism," reversing their previous position on the success of the Asian Dragons as being due to their draconian political structures, and proclaimed anew an old doctrine of corrupt and unaccountable "oriental despotism" operating in a smoky, opaque den of vice.[14]

There is nothing so certain but that the extent of the collapse of Asia, or at least the speed at which it occurred, took the financial world by surprise. Yet, while most admitted to being stunned by the extent of the fall, a few claimed otherwise. One of those few was the IMF, which subsequently imposed its strict mandates on many of the defeated Asian states. Included in IMF reviews of every nation's economy is an array of both positive and critical observations. After the crash, the IMF began pointing to their criticisms of Thailand, embedded in largely laudatory reports, and they claimed that they warned the Asian states all along and were ignored. Thailand, not without some resistance, was one of the countries that acceded to the pressures of Western governments and their international governing organizations. In exchange for aid, the state enacted a series of tax increases, budget cuts, and sell-offs of state industries. Imposing its strict policy decisions on the defeated Asian states, the IMF could now demand austere budgetary measures and demand that certain fiscal numbers play themselves out in Thailand and say that the governments were just going to have to "endure the pain," as it is perennially said.

The moral and ascetic value of enduring pain is common to many of the world's religions, and it is no less true in international monetary discourse, though there is a strange exchange by which bodily pain — what one would normally assume here means the millions of Asians who go jobless, homeless, and hungry — is transformed into a discourse of "political will" and "nerve," whereby "pain" is an almost quantifiable phenomenon that appears in budgets or, at most, is vaguely placed in the "body" of the state. And that body must reform its immoral ways by an ascetic regimen in which does not give in to the flesh . . .

The Flesh of the Number

Now, huddled in a rural Northern Thai valley in the house of a spirit, these body parts of the economy, whose pain state planners must endure, are, like the IMF, also in search of numbers, the right numbers. Here, as in most places in Thailand, there is an illegal black-market lottery, an underground trade in numbers that passes huge amounts of uncountable currency in an undocumented and unseen economy below any ground of economic reality that a forecaster's indicators could detect.

Now, as commentators universally accept the reality of the Asian contagion, the financial and equity markets for Thailand are, as they say, plagued with "risk aversion." Money has dried up. Banks have risk aversion. Investors have risk aversion. There is no money being lent to businesses that need it while investment retreats from Asia and elsewhere. The system depends on the taking of chances in the hopes of returns. And so risk aversion infects the very heart of capital.

By contrast, the time of misfortune and the hour of death in the Lampang countryside is a time for intense illegal gambling. Most funerals are an occasion for networks of relatives and friends to assemble on behalf of the dead and give the spirit a good sendoff. Monks are brought in to give chants to the dead. People bring presents of money to the family. Everyone eats — a lot — and cooperates in pulling off the event. And during the night, for several nights, people from all over the area turn out for the illegal gambling that goes on all night long around the corpse. Dice and roulette are the favorite illegal games, offered by professional dealers who tour the funeral circuit, giving a cut of their surplus take to the family of the dead. At the funeral this surplus giving to the family for the sake of the deceased is a high-prestige gift, a portion of which also becomes surplus giving over to the chanting monks as Buddhist alms, the good effects of which are also ritually transferred over to the dead. Here, the intense social relations made apparent, strengthened, and realized in the act of giving — quite in the spirit of how Marcel Mauss characterized the gift — are linked directly to the act of gambling, in which individuals seek maximum profits for their investments, certainly an ur-form of the spirit of capital as Marx characterized it, M-M¢ exchange, whereby the fetish value of capital appears to have the nature of self-reproductive increase, or as Benjamin Franklin advised the young tradesman, "Money begets money, which begets yet more."[15] In Lampang, in what I would call a "funeral casino," these two elementary forms of economic life — gift and capital — are not extricable one from the other.[16] The hour of death is a time for the intensification of exchange, the time of calamity and misfortune is the time to set caution to the wind and play games of pure risk and chance and at the same time work up that surplus value that is given over, in gifts to the family, to the Buddhist monks, and ultimately to the dead. The whole production is a massive aid package delivered in a time of need. Though there is no contract, it is socially understood that this is what one does should anything happen.

In economics, that function of backup at a time of unexpected misfortune has been called "moral hazard," a hotly debated idea in the wake of recent currency debacles. Originally arising out of the terminology used by insurance companies, moral hazard now refers more generally to the effect that is present in behavior when risk is backed up by real or imagined potential compensation. For instance, some time ago insurance companies easily discovered that if someone has insured, say, a horse against theft, he is statistically more likely to leave it around unguarded. And so it is with all other kinds of risk. With moral hazard in play, it is said, and knowing there is a safety net, individuals, corporations, even states, will take risks in that artificial and unnatural situation that otherwise would be economically irrational so long as they believe there is a structure in place to bail them out. In relation to state-level management of national economy, moral hazard is supposed to be an econometrically deadly combination by which businesspeople, seeking their self-interests, operate with extreme risk under the assumption that the state exists in patronage relation to their ventures in banking and finance and will rescue them should they not pay off. On an international level, discourses of moral hazard have been developing an audience steadily, especially since the establishment of the IMF. Fringe conservative elements (which always get a fair hearing in economic discourse) have been alerting the world to the dangers of international financial bailout mechanisms, such as the IMF, which encourage risky behavior that would otherwise be irrational without a fallback guarantor. Every country, each to its own, should stand or fall on the merits of its own policies. To encourage otherwise only enables unsound practices.

Such arguments should sound quite familiar, for ultraconservative positions are, in form, just as insistent in opposing state welfare or in opposing the IMF or other interventions as they are in opposing state management of economy. It is said that moral hazard, in all its forms, creates a distortion of reality: the familiar argument that any responsibility of the state or other collectives to individuals not only fails to help them but makes them worse, for it is an enabler of the inability to face up to what the hard realities demand. Such collective enterprises create artifices and unnatural environments that fail to pose the challenges that reality demands for the sake of the best adaptation to it.

With each global financial crisis that requires intervention, and with steadily mounting Third World debt tended or brokered by the World Bank and IMF, the discourse of moral hazard has expanded its audience from conservative and isolationist elements in the West to a more globally contentious reach. And the peak of moral hazard's prominence, at least so far, has been the Asian crisis. Here was a situation in which strong state management of economies had, vexingly, led to rapid economic growth. But eventually, with the decline, the moral authority of those states was rapidly divested, and it was pronounced that Asian corporations and financial institutions had engaged in wildly risky behavior as they had believed their states would bail them out. Therefore, it was argued, the international community should not intervene but let the Asian economies learn their lesson and adjust to the economic realities.

Just as importantly, the scramble of international governing organizations to do something about the currency crisis, and particularly the actions of the IMF, only fell further into the hands of those in the know as to what is really real about economy and what is unnatural and illusory. Following the sudden crash of some of the most widely lauded economies in the world, this struggle for influence after the Asian currency crisis was a question not only of moral authority but also of the very power to see into the reality of economy itself, of knowledge of economic reality as the precession to power over it. And this, I would venture, is often a question of prophecy. How do you see the future? How do you issue positive reviews of the Thai economy's future and at the same time have been right all along?

True Prophecy

For an answer to that problem, I would return you to that spirit altar in Northern Thailand where Thai gamblers, illegal lottery players, magic believers, and police bribers crowd around a woman possessed by a lucky spirit boy who has the good numbers. In the underground lottery, bets are taken locally, and any winnings are dispersed locally by certain dealers in a secretive and unsurveilled economy and traffic in numbers. Beyond the gaze of the state, beyond the world financial architecture, here in the spirit boy's shrine, the Thais grow a lavish money tree under which prophecies are issued at a rate approaching twenty per hour. These are true prophecies. There is no control over the winning numbers, which are entirely in the hands of the State Lottery Commission's official bimonthly drawing, whose numbers the underground lottery uses. After receiving their forecasts of this event, which is entirely beyond the control of the medium, the clients depart with their numbers. Winners always return with gifts of gold for the spirit when he is right.

How is the spirit able to do this? And was my transgression of the rules the reason no one made money with numbers which were, I have to admit, the right ones?

Since the crash, more and more people show up for the boy, and more and more win. The more he is right, the more people will come to him, and the more people come, the more numbers he passes out to each. So also — and here is the rub — the more numbers that are out there, the more chances there are of some of them being right. He does not give out the same numbers but a variety of them. In this way the spirit wagers his authority on many different numbers at the same time, and the more the better. And the more he turns out to be right, the more his authority grows. By virtue of increase, eventually even becoming the only game in town for prophecy, the prophet increasingly generates true prophecies, and all this without any control over the winning numbers. These are clearly not self-fulfilling prophecies. In effect, the spirit practically has a bet on all numbers but never puts money on any of them. It costs nothing to issue a prophecy. And most importantly, it is the prophecies that turn out to be true that are singled out visibly, in this case by the returns of gold and the miracle growth of the money tree.

In fact, and to this day, I still cannot say why I got the right numbers or why no one made any money off them, but what this means to the devaluation of the morality of the state in Asia is that at this critical juncture in which prophecy plays so crucial a part, one must wager prophecy to win out morally. How does transnational capital issue positive forecasts for Asia and still be right? Whether any particular econometric forecast is right or not is not as important as the fact that some must be right and that one must command the stage where those are seen to be so and where one can continue to issue forecasts, the more the better. In the production of such forms of prophetic authority, there is a constant, albeit thoroughly hedged, wager in play at all times, a gamble over the means, the ends, and the very nature of the economic real. It is defining the parameters of the economic real that is the true gambit here in order that one can control the idiom in which real economic prophecy is constituted and becomes the center of attention. That determines the strength of the audience you are able to convene, in effect, the multitude of casinos in which you may place your bet of prophecy and the variety of bets you may place.[17]

The fact that moral devaluation accompanies the project of monopolizing prophetic discourse can be seen, for instance, in the way in which the IMF explained the actual results of the Asian crisis, which far exceeded the very modest negative prophecies they wagered before the crash. IMF spokespeople, drawing on previously established tropes in economic discourse, talked of that which exceeded their forecasting as an "unexpectedly virulent contagion" that swept over Asian economies and on to the rest of the world.[18] While this was a previously existing metaphor in finance, the world media picked up on it sharply during the financial crisis and further popularized it as the "Asian contagion." In a classic discursive move, the phenomenon was reified as a cataclysmic fact of nature rather than as something man-made — a phenomenon to be observed and etiologically diagnosed as though the nature of its existence were unrelated to the observer. Strangely enough — though not so strangely when considering the ethnological ubiquity of moral interpretations of natural calamities — at the same time, this fact of nature can be attributed to a moral transgression by the first population that is imagined to have transmitted the virus to the others.

That which exceeded the expectations and forecasts of the IMF is a "Thai virus" born in a "go-go capitalism" that flouted its safety warnings. Like the classic explanations attached to magic, and as with my unplaced lottery wager, the explanation of failed divination is to be referred to moral uncleanliness or transgression. The IMF's modest warnings given beforehand actually prove then, not disprove, the magical and prophetic clear insight into the real of those who are now morally more suited to dictate the cure to the patient.

However, blinded by their own light, the IMF went on to blow their wad of moral capital on one failed, narrow bet on the cure.[19]

These tricks of prophecy indicate how irreality discourses at this crucial juncture in business are such a tricky business in themselves. Take, for an example, the proliferating discourse of irreality surrounding the US internet stock bubble, a call for consciousness of fundamental facts of the economic real that has been distributed for so many years through so many schools of stock analysis and financial investment. This critique is not one of fact apart from a will to power: while doubtless it is true that stock prices rose beyond realistic growth factors for profitability in those companies, at the same time it is important to realize that these realist assessments are voiced by a structure of elite business power that was threatened by new structures of capitalization that might swallow them up in so many "soft" AOL-Time Warner takeovers of the "hard" companies. Indeed, the oldest and most respected firms on Wall Street, in collusion with business media networks who carried their forecasters' buy signals, were behind the unjustified flood of IPO registrations and, in association with their agents, sold off their reserved stock and cashed out early, often by the end of the first day of IPO. After stock prices slipped out of control, the control over an unruly and unorthodox new internet market fell increasingly into the ownership and control of the central players in the old economy, advancing the centralization of capital, which has capped off every other up- and downswing in the US market and will go on later to cap off the 2008 one as well.

The same relations of power played themselves out in the Asian miracle/Asian contagion cycle, as Asian business models that were so enthusiastically supported in the upswing were in the downswing decried as irrational and irreal while their means of production were quickly snapped up by many of the same foreign investment sources that had set up the miracle growth after having cashed out early. The accompanying enforcement by international governing organizations of proper business models cements the deal as states and their management of civil economy are increasingly imbricated in a particular version of the rationality of the market.

This may be a crucial movement in the transformation of moral authority in Thailand, a trickle-down pass-off of the accursed excesses of the irrational and illegal to those with no access to the international structures that are increasingly pitting them against their own state and banishing them from the land of the economic real. It is the nature and meaning of the economic real that is at stake here, a bid to monopolize the terms in which economic prophecy is expressed and so to become the leading game in town.

4 · PROVE IT

MY THOUGHTS WERE DANGEROUS. When the other kids would go to play in the water or at the bank, I would not go with them. So I was more alone than ever. After the neighbor man died at the hands of the Tree Woman, and it was all my fault, I not only avoided talking about it but also avoided my precious creek. Not that this helped much. When they would go, I would wish and wish and wish that none of them die, none of them drown. If I got mad at any of the kids, I would go to the Buddha image in my home and kneel down and think of his loving kindness for everyone and send that out to everyone. At night, before I slept, I would do my prostrations in bed like my mother taught me and then wish and wish and wish that all the kids be safe, one by one by name, that all the grandmothers be safe and all the grandfathers and all the fathers and mothers and aunts and uncles. It took a long time before I was able to sleep. And I couldn't remember everyone every night and never knew where to draw the line. But no one I remembered ever died that night or the next day.

And in the day, when I got in fistfights with the boys, I would hit them hard. But afterward, I would think of them kindly, imagine how they were when they were little babies, vulnerable, scared little babies that needed love. That way I was keeping everyone safe.

It was a tremendous burden, a constant effort that I had to keep up day and night. It changed me. I became even more of a loner because it was difficult to really talk and laugh with people and focus on games or school, because I was always watching my mind for any hint of dark thoughts. They were dangerous. She might hear them. I had to keep everyone safe.

She. My one dark thought that I allowed myself was resentment and almost hatred for her. She had cursed me.

I wished I could be like Uncle Chai, who was actually one of the most pathetic people in the village and was rather mean. He wasn't my uncle, really, but as I told you, we kids always called any older man uncle. I wished I could be like him, because Uncle Chai didn't believe in anything to do with spirits and ghosts.

Although I was young, I still knew the difference between those who believe and those who don't. I was aware that I was the type of person for whom these things — *phiisangthevada*, ghosts and deities — were real even if they were invisible (most of the time). It's not like I was in some kind of weird reality. I was a normal person like anyone else, and in the daylight and while doing my various affairs of a little girl, I saw the world as a very plain place where rain fell from the sky because everything falls when dropped and does not float instead, where when you heard a voice, there was a live person attached to it who you could see and touch with your hand. I know that world, that reality, and it does not go away. It is just that there is more for me. Not all the time, though. When it is there, it is there, and when it is not, it is not. But for good old Uncle Chai, there was never anything more to life than this ordinary reality.

He had been to Bangkok on several occasions for his civil service training, and he believed himself — and let everyone know at every moment — that he knew what was really what in this world, in a way village bumpkins could not. But he was not in the civil service anymore. He had been demoted, kicked around, and finally kicked out by his malicious bosses for basically believing too strongly in the code of ethics and refusing to take bribes. This is what one gets for being such an antisocial hardhead, taking everything so literally.

But he still wore his uniform around the village despite the snickers he got all around. He drank rice rum every day, which made this bearable, and I think the drunkenness also changed the appearance of the worn-out uniform in his own eyes.

Uncle Chai loved Thailand more than life itself. He loved the king, and he loved King Rama V, the bringer of modernity to Thailand. And he was also a huge fan of Abraham Lincoln. Huge. Almost every day he would get drunk and tell all the children, over and over, about Abraham Lincoln, who had freed the slaves in America and valued the equality of everyone, and then he would begin crying, eyes wet and throat gagging for air, about this Abraham Lincoln, who in the end was shot in the back of the head.

Well, these are the pathetic things about Uncle Chai that I would think about when I got around to him in my nightly rounds of keeping everyone safe. I would not think about the other side to him, which is what got him into the trouble with the government service in the first place. The hard-headedness. He was a know-it-all, and the one thing he knew so much about, of which all these village bumpkins were ignorant, was on the subject of the existence of phiisangthevada, supernatural beings. Or, rather, the nonexistence of them.

When the neighbor man died from the Tree Woman attack, Uncle Chai scoffed and used it as a grand occasion to rail drunkenly at everyone for having their eyes cloaked in the darkness of superstition, unmodern and un-Buddhist, completely without basis and with no proof whatsoever. As the days and weeks passed, he ridiculed anyone who went out to the tree during the day to make offerings to it, which is, of course, what people started doing as soon as the first one of them was killed by it (and, of course, no one would go at night). They would pass by Chai carrying candles, lotus flowers, incense, rice rum, and sometimes a pig's head. And Chai would sit there in his worn-out civil service uniform, sipping rum and smoking, yelling at them, "Prove it! Prove it!"

They went out there whenever there was misfortune in a family, or just if they feared it, had bad thoughts about the gods and spirits, or did something bad that they thought might not be looked kindly upon. It was understood that it was a *jow thii*, a spirit of place, that inhabited the tree, and a powerful one. It must be very old, so old that it was almost forgotten, and now it had woken up, and it was mad. It was normal for trees to be inhabited by female spirits, but that this one was a woman spirit was a bit strange in that she was so powerful, and that is probably what scared everyone more than anything. But to Uncle Chai, the gender did not appear to matter. He was an equal-opportunity skeptic.

He challenged anyone in the village to prove to him that ghosts were real. And then, one especially drunken day, he declared to everyone that he would show them all. He had been living this life for forty-three years now, and he had never seen hide nor hair of any ghost. So he declared to everyone that he was going to sleep the whole night at the tree of the Tree Woman.

Immediately, of course, as is our way here in our village, everyone began to place bets. Because this happened all of a sudden, only Ba Jae (to whom I will return in a while), the queen of all the local moneylenders, had this amount of cash on hand to bankroll all the bets this way and that. Would Uncle Chai actually go through with it, or would he not? Would he see the Tree Woman, or would he not? Would he stay all night? Part of the night? What hour would he come back? An even number or odd? Would he survive this, or would he die?

Every permutation had a bet and specific odds. And no one knew that I, alone, had the power to tip them.

As Uncle Chai stormed off in the failing light, laughing at everyone and laughing to himself on his way, I went straight home to the Buddha image and began the *attitaan*, the wishing well for others that had been my yoke of late. I kneeled before the Buddha and thought about Abraham Lincoln, and this helped bring warm, kind feelings for Uncle Chai. I wished him well, wished him no harm.

And then, the story goes, as he walked into the forest and as he got into a small boat and began to paddle down the creek, an increasing dread began to rise in his bowels. The closer he got, the greater it became until it was not funny anymore.

I know that over where I was, I did not feel so great either. I felt it, too, in my guts. I had kept everyone safe. But no one had done anything like this yet, and I did not know whether I could keep him safe if he went straight *there*, the last place that I would ever go.

Well, before Uncle Chai even got within sight of the tree, he became so afraid that he turned back. He crept back and went to sleep the night at the house of a close kin, one who probably had a lot of money at stake. Then, very early, he snuck back to the edge of the forest and pretended to emerge out of it when everyone was up.

That next morning he proudly announced to everyone what fools they were and that he had shown them what to think about their country superstitions and that there are no such things as ghosts.

But when it was time to pay out, Ba Jae was having none of it. The village was teeming with people yelling this way and that, some people demanding their winnings, others refusing to pay, while only Uncle Chai was calm, laughing to himself, and Ba Jae barked down everyone coming at her. She had a booming voice. She was the richest woman in the area by far, at that time around forty-five years old or so, but to me she really looked more like sixty because she dressed so finely, because she was so confident, and especially because she was as unafraid of men as any older lady was. And probably because she had a lot of weight on her shoulders, managing all that money she had lent out all over the place, which also brought a lot of lines to her face. The money lenders say that to remain sane as a lender, you must be able to set your mind right with the attitude of kissing your money good-bye. But who can truly do that?

She was having none of this. Ba Jae had her eyes and ears in the village. And one of her people, no doubt someone in great debt to her, had followed Uncle Chai all the way (it must have been a big debt) and had seen exactly what he had done.

But before Ba Jae could get this story across to everyone, there was a huge commotion, and several fights broke out. One old man even went in his house to get a machete and began waving it around with a double grip that he had seen in Hong Kong kung fu movies, two skinny arms slicing the air in a most awkward and inefficient manner.

When they finally calmed down, everyone was furious at Uncle Chai. They started slapping him on his balding head, and his comb-over was sticking up in the air, his eyes watery, and then they started tugging on his civil service uniform. That was too much to bear, and Chai erupted into a fury of flailing fists in all directions. It was almost like he grew two extra arms.

"I'll show you! I'll show you!" Chai was screaming. People backed off, partly because he looked so funny with his hair poofed up and his uniform all disheveled. To save face, he would go to sleep at the tree, and this time there was no turning back. He would have to do it.

He got tipsy during the day, and by nighttime he was in good spirits again and laughing at everyone again. Bets were placed, adjusted. Odds were different. Uncle Chai went off laughing at his bumpkin neighbors, yelping over his shoulder, "Show me the ghosts, ha-ha!"

As the story goes, this time several people were following a few paces behind while others were waiting up ahead. Some were already in their small boats, waiting in the creek. As he passed them, he would laugh, saying, "Aren't you afraid of the ghosts?" And as it got darker and darker and they got closer and closer to the tree, indeed they were. The people thinned out, and sometimes for a stretch he was all alone.

I had gone home to meditate on Abraham Lincoln, but it didn't work.

Chai landed his boat on the bank and disembarked. There was one older lady there watching him, and he laughed, saying to her, "Aunt, aren't you afraid there are ghosts here?"

"Oh, I heard all about that. But I've never seen anything strange here," she said, chuckling too.

"Where are the ghosts, then!" he said, laughing a little more.

"Right!" she said, laughing harder. "I've been here and never seen one ghost! Ha!" She wasn't really looking at him though. She had her face turned toward the ground.

Chai looked down and couldn't see anything there. "What's wrong, Aunt? Did you lose something?"

"No, I'm just laughing. That's how I laugh about all this ghost silliness."

Chai chuckled in agreement. "All my life I have lived now, I have never seen a single ghost. So I've come here to finally see one. I am curious to see what they look like, hee-hee!"

"I've lived around here, too, and I have never seen a ghost even just once, either. I want some of the action!" And she started laughing with gusto.

"Yeah, if I see one, I'm going to kick it in the ass, ha-ha!" Chai laughed some more. It was a relief to find a kindred soul, and as he laughed more, she laughed more. It was like contagious giggling, but bigger. He couldn't stop laughing. He tried, but he couldn't control it. It was ridiculous that he couldn't stop laughing. At first, everything seemed so funny, him out here by the tree, and how silly that he had actually been afraid the night before. But then he couldn't stop this laughing, and that wasn't funny. He laughed, she laughed. She laughed, he laughed.

Things began changing. The more she laughed, the more difficult it was for him to see her through his teary eyes. As she laughed, she grew almost transparent, in a way, but also glowed white, and was looking straight at him.

"You said that if you see a ghost you are going to kick it in the ass! Ha, hee-hee!" On and on she laughed and laughed.

The more she laughed, the whiter and whiter she glowed. Suddenly, her face started to change, to become warped, the nose and chin and eyes out of proportion and twisted, and then her skin took on a sickly greenish hue.

Chai's laughs became deep groans from his belly, and he went limp and weak, and then passed out.

ơ The next morning we villagers found him at the foot of the tree. He was curled up in a ball like a baby and laughing at nothing, sometimes yelling out, "Prove it! Prove it!" and then bursting into tears. His condition didn't ever really improve.

After that, the bets were all paid out, fair and square. Uncle Chai spent the rest of his days in "cracked mindfulness," living on leftover alms at the temple, and was taken care of by the monks, who would wash his uniform for him once a week.

5 · REGENDERED DEBT

GREAT PAINS CAN BE TAKEN IN CORRECTING the perceptions of a certain kind of economic madness: a rather conventional question of the relation between a realm that is understood in some crucial sense as a fiction — abstract, ethereal finance, fetishized value, universalizing and spanning the globe without respect to geographical place, for instance — and what is real, the concrete, lived situations of real humans in their social embeddedness, cultural specificity, and locality.

The context of postcrashing Thailand may provide an occasion on which to explore this conventional dynamic given the ways in which local practices with money are threatened by, but also possibly threaten, the transformation of localities into a viable medium in which global capitalism can thrive.[1] It is possible to see local practices and ideas as possibly imbricated in, possibly in tension with, the reorganization of society into a globalization-friendly medium. For instance, one can see the power struggle at stake when a state does something like, say, legislate and enforce capital controls that impede or prevent the movement of transnational capital across borders, geographical or otherwise. But what is at stake in localities that are less defined and organized by the work of formal state laws or institutions? They are, in one sense, more vulnerable to the state law when it acts as mechanism of larger global imperatives and, in another sense, are more difficult to shape, are more diffuse and flexible to the degree that they exist, in part, beyond that kind of law by definition.

There are important frameworks for the architecture of finance in Northern Thailand that are, like the prophetic moral authority of spirit mediums in the gambling economy and like the social security system in funeral casinos, irregular financial instruments that offend the current definitions of commonsense morality, and consequently also legality, and are in the process of entering a state of siege, as their eradication is, I would argue, absolutely critical to the integration of local economic practice in Thailand with the expanding influence of transnational funds of capital. And yet the question of whether this story of the cultural infiltration of abstraction, of neoliberal or financialized forms of life, can penetrate as easily in life as it can seem to do in theory, is something worth asking, especially in locales that are no strangers to abstraction in matters of life or money or debt.

In Thailand, that which I am speaking of here goes generally under the apt rubric of *gnun nawk rabaub*: "out-of-the-system money," meaning debt and credit instruments that are beyond national accounting and control mechanisms. Like gambling and spirit forecasting, they carry connotations of impropriety and are — especially now — a subject of deep concern to the ministry of finance and other agencies. Moreover, they exist in a symbiotic relationship with gambling and other moral economies on the local level.

The Godmothers

Some of the most important conduits for money in the Lampang countryside are individual lenders who work out of the home, called *jow mae gnun goo*, or "loan godmothers."[2] Their primary client base is composed of market vendors (primarily women), those needing a boost of cash due to misfortune or for periodic large-scale outlays such as school tuition for children, habitual gamblers as well as funeral casino dealers, and other godmothers in need of short-term liquidity. Clients use personal connections or the vouching of friends to approach the loan godmothers and request loans, typically ranging anywhere from the equivalent of $100 to $3,000. They sign papers for the payment of a legal 15 percent per annum interest rate, but the amount borrowed is left blank, allowing the true interest rate — typically 6 percent per month — open to calculation retrospectively should the affair go to court. And whenever possible they hand over their ATM cards and codes to the godmothers for the monthly minimum extraction, which is interest only.

The loan godmothers are organized into *wong*, or circles ("wong" is also the word for the traditional form of circular public dancing). Each wong is started by a successful godmother who brings friends and relatives into the circle, showing them the ropes of contracts and lawyers should anything go wrong, handing out advice for avoiding problems, and introducing clients when the founding godmother is too extended. These are lifelong associations, not necessarily mutually exclusive but tending to settle into stable socializing patterns, which also facilitates the trust necessary for extending special lending rates to one another. Each wong, in turn, has a fuzzy circumference in that godmothers accept deposits widely from kin and friends, usually yielding 3 percent a month, or half the retail rate. The wongs also gather for ostentatious collective charity works, typically the funding of schools and temples.

The local public perception of the godmother circles is ambivalent. Tolerated and widely relied upon, based in personal relations, the network of lending with godmothers is nevertheless also considered impersonal and extractive and, at least when projected against the most idealistic standards, appears as selfish and self-interested. What they are doing can ultimately be reduced to being, at base, immoral. "They make their living on the backs of others," it is said. But the moral economies in play in the area are complex and contradictory. The operations of loan godmothers are essential to the local economy. Few people in small-time enterprise, for instance market vendors or dice dealers, have access to official lending from credit corporations, and certainly the recently swelling ranks of the unemployed who seek to start something up have no such access. As in big business, maintaining or expanding a livelihood in the market is often impossible, especially since the postcrash inflation, without access to credit. And much of the entire rural population, entrepreneurial or not, has no feasible cushion should they face misfortune apart from what can be organized on the local level. While godmothers are not considered overly virtuous, and while their practices are certainly illegal, at the same time this questionable virtue demands that they participate, like spirit mediums, in public works. Godmothers themselves sometimes speak to me in ways that barely conceal a simmering guilt. And certainly the borrowing public, at least, think this is the case, given their frequent gossip about the godmothers' fear of curses and their consequent desire to earn good *kamma* for themselves through giving.

The godmothers, like national banks, trade in reputation: in their case, especially their reputations for having cash on hand as well as reputations for sticking to agreements and reputations for giving back to the community. Despite the associations that might be aroused by my English translation of "jow mae" and its evocation of the Mario Puzo mafioso, godmothers use only legal contracts and have no means for threatening violence and are often resigned to losing a portion of their capital. Because lending arrangements are most often in some way based upon social connections, there are many spheres of kinship and friendship relations at stake in any loan. And the public reputation of the individual borrower is also at stake in this out-of-the-system money, as, by definition, the borrower who goes out of system has little other than his social standing to stand on as collateral and can face excommunication from the local money market should he default.

Just as life for the rural person of modest means periodically demands outlays of large quantities of capital in order to meet basic needs like education and health care, so, too, does the local economy in affordable basic food essentials depend upon the maintenance of numerous small-time vendors in the markets that pepper the villagescape of the countryside, in each case necessitating access to finance capital. And just as the risk-averse stagnation of lending in medium and large domestic businesses presents a fundamental obstacle to recovery in the documented economy, the undocumented local economy is equally threatened by the new economic conditions, and the godmothers provide the means to keep that economy going—or at least slow its demise.

The other major market in money instruments is, of course, the field of public gambling, which is perhaps where the fastest and most explosive action in monetary circulation occurs. Habitual gamblers would have to quit, at least periodically, without access to a cushion after taking a large hit, or worse, their families would have to do without in that regular eventuality. Small-time dealers as well would have to hang up their mats after a single bad night. Then people would die without a casino in their honor, spirits would be unhappy, and families would face extreme hardship after the deaths of economically essential members. And, similarly, the godmothers themselves would eventually lose an important sector of their clientele, thus creating liquidity problems, ruining their reputations, and they would have to turn people — whatever their reason for coming — away at the door.

And circulating around these overlapping circles of exchange are monks and spirit mediums, who provide services of divination and prophecy and who are both the recipients of gifts and important nodes for rechanneling wealth in the form of public works. While monks are officially prohibited from forecasting, spirit mediums (mostly women) are unofficial clerics who have until recently been unfettered and so have issued, in great volume, prophecies and talismans of good luck that both gamblers and others use to negotiate their way through the mazes of money and other vulnerable aspects of life. Monks and spirits create the conduits through which the market of irregular financial instruments can remain tapped, in part, into a moral economy that both curbs excess extraction and rechannels wealth at the same time that it eggs people on, whether for the sake of the dead or because the dead intervene for the sake of the living. Spirit mediums in particular cultivate the climate of confidence and optimism that is necessary for speculators to embark on their ventures. In matters of money and lucky numbers, spirit mediums reign supreme in terms of both civil freedom and perceived efficacy. Particularly because gambling is not considered a purely virtuous activity, to put it mildly, it is, of course, spirits (those who come back with a powerful thirst for life) rather than monks (ostensibly world renouncers) who are seen as most likely to lend the avaricious living an advantage at the table.

Now, there is one thing that I have not emphasized enough about this essential, complex web of interdependent financial instruments, and that is the fact that the most important conduits of exchange in this out-of-the-system money course between women. The wong of godmothers takes deposits from men, but they are almost always kin, whereas a wide circle of female friends can deposit with a godmother, and deposits with godmother wongs are frequently used by women to hide savings from their husbands, thereby protecting those savings. Spirit mediums are mostly, but not exclusively, women, and dice game operators, at least at funeral casinos, are almost invariably women. Gamblers are women by a slight majority, while gamblers who borrow from godmothers are about equally men and women, as are those who borrow for personal emergencies and large-ticket expenses, while the majority of borrowers for small venture capital are almost all women, as reflects the fact that local market vending is mostly controlled by women. And so I am suggesting that not only is this money market essential to the local economy, it is particularly essential to the welfare and power of women.

And it has been this way for some time.

POOR UNCLE CHAI, the drunken ex–civil servant, refused to let even a little of the beyond into his sense of the real, and so instead it came all of a sudden — too fast, too much — and his mind cracked. Whimpering under the tree, barely able to tell everyone of the horrors he had seen there that night.

I myself have sunk, in my own way, into the darker places of the mind. But I have never had that hard a shell around my mind. And I never, as we put it, "cracked my mindfulness." Well, maybe just a hairline crack. Overall, unfortunately, my sanity was right there with me all along, taking everything in the whole time.

This is after I got my "job" protecting the whole village from my thoughts and coming up with lottery numbers for my mother. For a while, there was nothing good in my life, until one of my uncles died (a different uncle, not Gongkam, about whom I do not want to speak right now). All of us kids were to ordain, to make merit for his departed spirit by (temporarily) going forth into homelessness as *samanera*, novices in the Buddhist order. Well, not all of us kids. Or, rather, just not me.

Seeing as I was a girl, I was not permitted to ordain as a samanera nor, for that matter, later as an adult *bhikkhu*. Samaneri and bhikkhuni no longer existed in Thailand or any of the other Theravada Buddhist countries, having died out by neglect a thousand years earlier, with no women left to pass down the ordination to the others. Or that is how the authorities describe it. Others say this is a minor technicality and that the real reason is a reluctance to give up the patrimonopoly.

I cried and cried. I would not eat or speak. I really screamed, furious and desperately hurt. Finally, after several days of driving everyone mad, on the day of the cremation, they told me I could ordain as a boy novice, for a day, to get me to stop torturing them with my cries.

My head and eyebrows were shaved, as were those of the boys, and since I was prepubescent and wearing the white robes of a *naga*, or one about to go forth, I finally looked just like a boy.

I was ecstatic. So happy, the happiest moment of my life. So happy, so at home, finally at home. But it did not happen the way I expected. I was only allowed to ordain as a little white-robed naga, and they never gave me the full ordination. I cried and cried, but still, I would not let them take the robes off me later.

When the funeral was over and the smoke cleared, they had to forcibly remove the robes from me before people started asking questions about what they were up to, ordaining a girl naga. Of course, I looked about the same as a little *mae chi*, or white-robed nun, which was not a real bhikkhuni and was perfectly legal. Or maybe I was ordained a mae chi, and they had tricked me. Naga, the white-robed boy, was our customary ceremony before real Buddhist ordination. Actual ordination of girls or women was most illegal, and even a naga ordination might stir up talk. But I had little appreciation of the importance of that fact. I only knew this horrible, twisted feeling, only the terrible injustice, the horrible, well . . . death, really . . . that I experienced the day my aunts — and I think my mother, too (it is such a blur) — held me down and took the white robes from me.

This was the big turning point in my life. After that, I was a sullen girl of extremely low energy and spirits. It took months before I would talk much or even eat much. They had to perform many blessing rites on me, calling my spiritual energies back into my body and sealing them in by tying blessing strings on my wrists and around my head, neck, and ankles.

The sinking feeling that struck me after the robes were torn off me and I was torn from the closest place I ever got the Buddhist order — it was too much for me to be able to bear, almost even to speak of now. Everything full of cool water and calm wind in my body had drained out of me, and all it left me with was *that*.

I can't explain how much it hurt, not clearly. That. The pain feels as though there is a poison running through your blood, a sour, metal poison. That. You sink onto the mat on the floor; your body is an alien and noxious thing, like it is attacking you from the inside.

It is metallic. That is the best thing I can say. Like metallic shavings, what it would be like to swallow, chew, and taste metal shavings, only it is your whole body that is churning in revulsion from the inside with this awful taste, your whole body tasting it, but not even just your whole body but its innermost sense, deeper than in the bones but also pervading the whole.

This fold, this inside of the inside of the body, erupting from within with this stinging metallic poison — it is maybe not even the body I am speaking of but just the feeling or the screen or plane in which feelings occur. That screen within the within of the inner body was itself screaming with this noxious, metal, alien taste.

The worst thing about it was I didn't even feel like I was dying. Instead, it seemed as though this could progress without limit, and I would be forced to be there with it all along to endless intensities and folds within folds.

In those days I was periodically hooked up by blessing strings to rows and rows of chanting monks, and a small fortune was spent on donations to sponsor the attempt to bring my spirits back into my body. They considered me to have been possessed. They decided that I had indeed been possessed by a malevolent spirit. They simply had not recognized it earlier. Despite my denials, they would not listen to me.

On my worst days, I would tremble and shake, sweat and black out. My relatives would tell me I that I spoke nonsense with a weird look in my eyes, of which I remembered nothing. The neighbors would say it was an ancient Northern Thai tongue and that a spirit had called me.

I thought at the time that possession was the perfect explanation, in their minds, for what they had done: they had ordained the male spirit that was in my body. They had never ordained me, a girl, and so had never actually done anything wrong. They had done nothing approaching an illegal act according to the governmental national law that governs the Buddhist clergy and, more importantly in their minds, had done nothing to violate the religion. Not that the law would recognize the male spirit in me, but the fact that they did themselves was enough for them to feel okay about what they had done or, rather, had not, in fact, done.

On my better days, as I walked down the red-dirt roads of Sala Village, I was always alone, and that is when Ba Jae took an interest in me. Of course, she had an interest in everything, a finger in every pot there was in Sala Village in those days. And I was a conspicuous part of the village even as a little girl. I would walk around in the sun in the intense heat without an umbrella. I would walk in the rain without an umbrella. It's not that I couldn't feel the elements or suffer from them but that it was almost as though it was not me who was feeling all those things, as though that were someone else, and what I was, was the one who was sinking with the barren, poison feelings within.

Actually, it was kind of funny in a way, looking back, at least when the Catholic nuns in my school would punish me. My father paid a lot of money to send me to a Catholic school over the mountain in Lampang Town, and then, while I was over there, the nuns would punish me for not paying any attention to what they, or anybody, were saying or doing. Of course, to a degree, every kid was like that, ignoring the references to Jesus, which were never mixed in with academic subjects. They never converted a single one of us, and I guess that was not their plan. But more or less all day long I would be ignoring them, so they would make me kneel in the hot sun out in the courtyard as a punishment, and little did they know that they could never get to me that way because the sun could never get to me. The sun could never reach where I was.

Ba Jae took me in and was the first to find me where I was. I think, actually, it was an umbrella in the sun that she offered me, but not by saying anything. Just walking up next to me and holding it over my head. It was suddenly cool, very cool. Not just on the outside. Inside, the cool breeze in my body returned for a few instants.

Ba Jae was the biggest jow mae, the biggest "godmother" lender in the area. The queenpin of outer Lampang. I didn't know at the time what it was about her that had reached me. Perhaps it was that to us villagers she was like a movie star, the most famous person in the area, the richest, the grandest. To be so close to greatness, it overwhelmed me.

Or maybe it was her energy, I thought, energy that was the opposite of mine at the time. She always moved in leaps and bounds, twitches and jerks, sways and bounces. It clashed with her expensive and shiny silk clothes, which were those worn by stately and reserved people of class. But being around her flashing and twitching, the life started to come back into my body, the cool water feeling, the calm breeze feeling. The alien, poison body, which seemed so real at times, more real than real, more real than everyday life and more real than anything I ever experienced, while I was around her, it would become just a memory, which if I tried to specifically recall exactly how it felt, felt almost as though it did not seem real at all but was rather some extravagant, imagined overreaction or invented memory.

To me, it felt something like a mother-and-daughter thing. Ba Jae had no children, and I knew that. It was like I would be a sort of child to her.

What she did have were two husbands and one extra lover, which everyone knew. What only she and I knew was that I was a secret agent who was to keep tabs on all of them. Doing my duty to her. Ba Jae was a busy woman, as the foremost jow mae in the area, with hundreds of loans out, hundreds of money schemes hatching, thousands of connections and relationships to manage, most of which were, of necessity, abstract in nature and could not involve much personal interaction. She had started as a gambler at the hi-lo mats in funeral casinos, ad hoc casinos that spring up around the corpse when it is brought home for at least a few days, or more, of Buddhist rites. She did well and soon was lending out her surplus winnings to other gamblers and to hi-lo dealers at handsome interest rates. One thing led to another until a circle of other successful gamblers and dealers popped up around her and began their own lending operations. Ba Jae was the queen of them all, however, always ready to back them if they needed and sometimes giving them cut-rate loans, which they, in turn, lent out. Eventually she had an interest in almost everything going down in and around the village, and had acquired a lot of land, some of it titled, and a lot of land of more intermediate status, including even the land down by the creek, of which the Tree Woman was jow thii, the place-lord, or owner in another sense.

Thankfully, I was not, at first, to watch over Ba Jae's land, or *that* land. I was to watch her men. This was the first interesting activity in several months that I actually performed in the world of the rest of the humans, of which I was, at the time, still a part.

The fact that the one man who had really crossed me, my neighbor, died a gruesome death at the hands of the Tree Woman — it never crossed my mind that this could have anything to do with Ba Jae's interest in me. But later I realized that it had everything to do with it.

Well, Ba Jae had married by arrangement when she was seventeen, neither young nor old for a woman back in those days. Actually, it maybe was a bit younger than average but not younger than what parents hoped for their daughters. That was Husband Number One. Husband Number One, at the time I began spying, had big bushy eyebrows that were graying, and he was about thirteen years older than Ba Jae, maybe fifty-eight. He had a cold and distant look in his eyes, and he never got upset about anything. While it was certainly humiliating for him to be a man whose wife was obviously "cheating" on him, he was just as content to accept the regular flow of money that came his way through his connection to Ba Jae. He, too, had women, I discovered, as well as a minor army of men who would dote on him for beer, rum, cigarettes, and small loans, for which he rarely asked repayment.

Husband Number Two was, of course, younger than Ba Jae. As her "minor husband," Number Two also had to accept, to a degree, a rather humiliating status. Although it was said that he joined her for love, not money, by the time I joined Ba Jae's operation, he was clearly in it for the money, at least in some part. He was a very handsome man, even at almost forty or something, and had many older women and widows, and many young ones as well, enraptured by his looks even though they also said he looked like a girl and there were rumors that he was gay. His diminished status as a minor husband was further compounded when Number Three joined the scene. Though Number Three was not what you could consider a minor husband but rather a frequent rendezvous, I will call him Number Three for the sake of continuity.

7:00 AM   Number One gets up, late. He has superhuman abilities to remain asleep during Army Radio broadcasts, which literally shake the timbers of the village every morning and blast out of the cackling loudspeakers of the village headman. He goes to the outhouse, wearing only a *pakauma* cloth wrap with half a relit cigarette, where he grunts out his morning constitutional and pours cold, cold water over himself for a shower.

7:45 AM   Number One heads out on his bicycle, peddling on the red-dirt road that leads out to rice fields and the pool hall. Funny, the pool hall would not be open this early.

8:00 AM   Number Two is still asleep. He looks like a baby sleeping. I peer through the cracks between the teak boards of his house and watch him sleeping there for some time. He turns over several times and stretches like a cat, enjoying the feeling and contentedly finding rest again. His room is very neat and organized. Shirts in one pile, neatly folded, pants in another. I can see his wallet there also, which is thick with money.

8:25 AM   Number Three is up already. He is dressed already. He is in a hurry. This time I try to follow, since he is on foot, and note that he is walking quickly through the village, looking into the balcony of almost every house. When he has toured practically the whole village, he goes to the tree across from Ba Jae's house, lights a cigarette, and sits there watching it while greeting and chatting with men and women passing by on their way to the fields or to their daily business.

On and on it would go like that. They were all late risers, which made my job easier. Every one of them, Numbers One through Three, would be doing curious things, and no wonder I was supposed to keep track of them. And yet just watching from the outside like that, I never did figure out on my own what they were up to, and it didn't mean anything to me. But it seemed to mean a lot to Ba Jae, who would put her hand (so surprisingly soft!) on mine and ask me to back up, tell it again, at various points some of which involved what seemed like perfectly ordinary details. She was getting increasingly worried. The lines on her face deeper, sadder, more afraid. She twitched and jerked around less and less and was more and more still.

She didn't explain it all to me at the time, but it all came together later, most of it.

The trouble started at night, with the funeral casinos. There were maybe five thousand people in our village and its environs. Of course, I didn't know them all, and when it was time for sleep and I had to wish each one well to keep them safe from the Tree Woman, I couldn't keep them all safe. I would forget people, even those I knew well, or I would drop off to sleep. So, despite all my efforts, sometimes, naturally, people died. And when people die, we take them home for several nights, ideally seven, for chanting monks, feasting neighbors, and all-night gambling around the corpse, mostly on dice games laid out on several mats, hosted by dealers for whom funeral casinos were their main livelihood. And most of the dealers were backed by Ba Jae or someone in her circle. You need a large stake to get your start in this profession, and you need a safety net should things take an unusual turn. Most dealers were in debt to Ba Jae since her interest rate, 6 percent per month, ate up a good deal of the profits, and then people always have other things they want to do with the rest of the money rather than pay on the principal of a debt, which is, after all, a rather abstract thing in their lives compared to so many immediate attractions. And funeral casinos were not the only games in town (that becomes important to relate later). Dealers often put their profits straight into other money schemes (which were not unconnected to Ba Jae either).

And, as I said, sometimes there are strings of luck for the gamblers, which is most unfortunate for a modest dealer. In fact, eventually, such a dip is bound to happen to everyone, so everyone is bound at some point or another to take a second or third loan from Ba Jae.

So strings of luck can be good for Ba Jae. But not if they happen all at once.

And that is exactly what happened after Gongkam died and his friends made the pact with his spirit.

Gongkam must have been sitting over their shoulders, just as he had promised to do during the spirit possession. Night after night Gongkam's friends would break first this dealer then that one. Of course, few people knew what was going on at first, but whatever they had settled on with Gongkam was definitely working.

There were three of them, the main culprits: Lert, Sert, and Noon. Iy Lert and Iy Sert were half-brothers with different fathers, both from Bangkok, each abandoned by his mother, a still-beautiful, almost unnaturally beautiful, hairdresser in town. They were scrawny, skinny boys who grew up wild and were your basic ne'er-do-wells, smoking, drinking, womanizing gamblers in need of a shave and haircut, the kind who so often get their just comeuppance in horror movies. Iy Noon, the third culprit, was a momma's boy and the son of a local merchant and was spoiled rotten. It was believed that he had simply fallen in with the wrong crowd, as it were, but, in fact, he had an insatiable appetite, and it was no accident at all that he would be drawn to and cast in his fate with the thrill seekers in town.

They hit funeral after funeral, in Sala Village and all the neighboring villages. And as the story goes — the story of the most incredible streak of luck ever seen in outer Lampang — in a span of a few weeks just about every dealer had to come running to Ba Jae for her implicitly promised loans. By the end of this period she was fully extended, as was everyone in her circle. Even cheat dealers could not defeat the trio, they say.

Of course, everyone suspected supernatural powers, and it was not long before the story of the seance emerged: of how the three ne'er-do-wells had promised Gongkam they would take his body back from the forest and (so some stories went) avenge him on his sister, Ee Nieo, and in return Gongkam would help them win big in gambling. In fact, I may have been the first to report the stories to Ba Jae. Since Gongkam was one of my uncles and Ee Nieo one my aunts, I heard the stories soon enough.

It was a surprisingly short time before Ba Jae was at her cash limit, had called in all debts she could, and had borrowed from friends all that she could. All she had left were her land holdings. Her whole enterprise was on the line because of these three jokers.

Or it seemed like only three (plus Gongkam) at the time. I, of course, was naturally drawn to the importance of my assigned spying tasks and so was certain that there was more to it all and that the key lay with one of the three husbands.

8:45 AM   Number One has already gone off on his bike ride to the middle of nowhere, and I am instead following Number Two. He is dressed smartly and neatly as always. His hair is greased like Elvis's. Despite his clothes and do, he climbs in the bed of the big truck that transports voyagers to Lampang Town on a most dusty ride through a small mountain pass.

10 AM   Number Three is keeping up his rounds, seeming to search for something or on the lookout against something at almost every house in the village.

12 NOON   Number One has returned from his bike ride, exhausted and sweaty. He takes another shower with a pail of cold water and sleeps out the afternoon in a deep, loud slumber.

3 PM   Number Two strolls back into town. He has not a speck of dust on him, and is wearing new, clean clothes. He has a small case with him. He walks in a strange, aimless pattern through the village roads, and I start to get the feeling he has noticed me.

I see that he has gone down the path behind the *wat*. Knowing where it comes out, I switch directions and run as fast as I can the long way around. At first I am really tired and breathing hard. I realize I will never make it, that he will disappear with that case and I will have failed Ba Jae. That the whole circle of women will be ruined and our whole world in the village will change; we will all be poor, and it is all my fault because I cannot run fast enough. But then everything changes, and without my noticing how it happened, suddenly I am bounding down the paths without any effort whatsoever as though I am a spectator and my body runs itself like a machine or a crazy puppet.

As I round the last corner, I see it. The heel of one foot disappears behind the corner of an old wooden fence. It is the heel of a nice leather shoe. A Western shoe, like Elvis might wear. I know where he has gone, to the house of Iy Lert and Iy Sert, who are often visited by Iy Noon.

I find a tree to climb, and although I dare not get close enough to peer into the cracks of their house, it is good enough to see comings and goings. They spend a very short time together, and then Number Two heads straight home again.

That night the three gamblers have more money than ever to place down on bets, and I see at least part of the secret to their unnaturally swift rise in fortunes. They have an overwhelming amount of cash on hand in comparison to the modest holdings of the dealers. It is not all coming from winnings recycled into bets. They have outside backers. Gongkam is not the only outsider ruining Ba Jae.

This, I feel, is the conclusion that Ba Jae herself arrived at following my reports, though she would rarely share her interpretations with me.

Of course, whether or not I could prove to myself that there was more behind the winning streak, eventually much more became attached to it, quite openly and explicitly.

The town became dry, starved for money, as these three jokers sucked the life out of us and through only funeral casinos and all the interconnected loaning and relationships brought into play to fund this extraordinary streak of luck and perhaps also the help of a downturn generally in the country. At first no one but Ba Jae and I had any idea of how pressed she was by outsiders to the village and by outsiders to the living. Eventually the market ladies would come for loans and be turned away by Ba Jae and her circle of lenders. And the customers began to dwindle as well, as everyone was also in some way connected to the funeral and gambling and lending economy. It was like the spirit was being drained out of the whole area as Iy Lert's gang took the money and spent it somewhere far way or sent it there.

Then strange men showed up in the marketplace in pairs. They started on the women in the local marketplace who used Ba Jae's network for small loans to fund their food stalls, their meat stalls, their fried-banana dessert stalls, their noodle stalls. But, of course, now Ba Jae's circle was in disarray and dry. The men offered unlimited loans but at high interest. Eventually the market news of the loans spread to the gamblers and dealers. Many people fell into it.

Naturally, when Ba Jae's game had become diminished, a new game in town would have to emerge in the vacuum. That is when the godfathers stepped in.

It was Bangkok money, everyone was sure, though it was administered through a network established in Lampang Town and headed up by a very powerful local power broker with national and Bangkok connections. I would love to further specify what I mean by "power broker," but that would give away too much identifying information to ones in the know, and that cannot happen in print just now.

Soon it became apparent that the pairs of men were teams of collectors imported from Bangkok and faraway provinces who could get rough if need be with the local debtors. They didn't have any local personal relationships. And this did happen, at first in a minor way. Many people soon could not keep up with the payments while others began to work only to keep up the payments and no more.

I could tell when someone fell into this situation. As things went sour in our town, so, too, did things start to go weird for me again. The people at the end of their wits with the new money lenders — I could see it in their faces, like anyone could, but what was different was that I could also feel it, a feeling like the person was not really fully there, sort of half-empty. And then I began to get the sense that I could see through people, that they were transparent.

Even Ba Jae herself was becoming weak in that way. Her jerky energy showed up less and less. Her money was running out. She began to appear transparent to me. Everyone's money was running out. It was like her feeling extended to the rest of the village. The little village shops did less business. The funeral casinos had less volume. There was less money everywhere. New houses were not being built. Money for seeds, fertilizer, and insecticide became harder to find. They went to the government credit union for special farming loans, which had various conditions, like you had to plant this or that, and those were always the bad ideas of experts in the government, and it never worked out. After several months it was clear, at least to me, that people had become more sullen in the day, more drunk and quarrelsome at night. Maybe it was just me, but not only did I see this, I felt it. Anyone could see that there was no one eating noodles at the noodle shop, that people did not have much for sale on their mats in the market, and there were not as many people there to buy, anyway. But I not only *saw* this, I could *feel* it, like it was part of me, like I was part of a bigger thing, a bigger body that was also sick.

No wonder that people fell into the daily loans.

Today, years later, people say that without the deal made with Gongkam, the godfathers would never have come. If they had not learned of the supernatural winning streak, they would not ever have come to outer Lampang and they would have had no way, money-wise, to get to anyone.

But they were not content to simply infiltrate the market in loans. They also wanted the land. It started with the money market but quickly shifted to our land. Land was where the future lay. Anyone could see that from a cursory examination of the cases of Japan and Korea. Of course, most local people who lived on, owned, or had some legally tenuous claim on land had little knowledge of this. But Ba Jae knew. She knew how ten years could easily mean more than a tenfold or twentyfold or even hundredfold increase in value. However, there was no way for her to get this across to everyone, especially once she became overextended. People were listening to the outsiders now.

And what the outsiders were telling them was that they could make thousands of baht off their land right then. Far more than they had ever gotten by selling and buying among themselves. It was the one spark of hope and ray of life. The only thing was, the buyers were not interested in a patchwork of little rice fields and plots strewn here and there. They wanted big spans of land, and anyone who wanted to sell would have to persuade his neighbors to do so as well.

That is when the big meetings started. When people started roping in and pressuring their kin and friends to sell land for thousands of baht, land that would be worth millions today. The clay in the soil was excellent. Not only was land an amazing speculative venture but the land, the earth of it, was itself, in its material properties, valuable matter for a ceramics industry as well as for housing on-site factories that could be populated by villagers who, without land of their own, would be obliged to work for wages.

But the best clay was down by the creek, where there were also big trees that could be cut down and sold, secretly, one at a time, where there was clear water to use in factory ventures and in which to drain out the residues. And the creek bed and all the big trees were almost all possessed by Ba Jae.

Many of us blamed this all on Gongkam's spirit, but I wonder whether it was not rather an inevitable development, that this sickness would have come and spread, would have happened one way or another. And yet, at the same time, no one at all knew better than me that the story that they tell about this time, about the ghosts and the Tree Woman and about myself, happens also to be true. Without the ghost luck, Ba Jae's position would never have become weak in the way that it did. It was Gongkam's ghost that opened the gate to the local money market for the godfathers. It was a ghost that first brought the daily loans to our out-of-the-way place.

If only Gongkam's elder sister, his own flesh and blood, had given him the money to fix his truck.

And the godfathers never did completely fade from the scene ever again.

7 · THE GODFATHERS

THE DISCOURSE OF GNUN NAUK RABAUB, "out-of-the-system money," which had, after the crash of 1997, become the focus of moral question and disciplinary action on the national level — and as I will show, by extension, on the transnational level — actually does not make any distinction between the circle of godmothers and all other kinds of undocumented lending.

Another form of available credit competing in the local finance market is called "the daily loan" and is available to almost anyone with few or no questions asked at a rate of 5 percent per day, payable daily. These notorious loans are secured through agents of regional crime syndicates, usually headed by the families of powerful national politicians. The debt collectors are men hired from faraway provinces and imported into the area to ensure that no social attachments impede daily collection, for which the maximum grace period is usually only one extra day. The collectors ride in teams of two, pillion on motorcycles, wearing uniforms, and make their rounds daily, house to house. Their primary client base is market women, who often need capital on short notice to keep up stocks of fish, meat, vegetables, cooked food, and other goods with low profit margins that require a continuous and perishable supply. Market women typically have no documented income, and if loan godmothers have no funds available or if the sellers are insufficiently integrated in women's friendship networks, small-time vendors have no way to access other sources in the formal or informal credit pool. Bodily harm, then, is their collateral.

While a daily payment of 500 baht ($17 USD) on a loan of 10,000 baht ($333 USD) can, in the best of times, be barely manageable, often that 500 baht represents the entirety of a day's profit, and sometimes more. A perpetual cycle of debt to the godfathers is the fate of many market women if they cannot get access to the loan godmothers or if the circle, wong, of lenders is fully extended. But that was not the only angle from which market vendors were under attack, especially after the crash.

One of the fastest-growing industries, one of the *only* growing industries in Thailand after the crash, was the megamart chain-store industry, which was funded by partnerships with foreign companies. These huge discount stores — typically at least as large as any Walmart in the United States — provide a market form contained within walls and owned mostly by European corporations, and through special bulk contracts with suppliers are able to offer goods at lower prices than local market vendors. They can also dump goods at a loss at will, tightening the noose on small-time vendors. Moreover, they can extend credit to the relatively well off while market women are often debtors. Nationalistic gestures of concern are made at the government level, but these megamarts were obviously courted by the government in recent years for two important reasons. Of course, the foreign investment creates a short-term improvement in the exchange balance. But even more important, the consumer transactions at these megamarts are all documented and so subject to taxation. Now, expanding the tax base is a primary concern of the IMF, which — retractions notwithstanding — continues to be obsessed with public sector debt. Not only is "value-added tax" (VAT) a most important feature of the deals cut with the IMF but, interestingly, since it is — on a macro level — a brake on domestic infratrade, it also increases the dependence on exports for economic recovery, which also remains the IMF's policy. But the sales tax is not only important for transnational creditors; it is of equal importance for those with stakes in the national money market as the new government prepares to transfer the disastrous private sector debt, largely from failed finance companies tied to failed real estate companies, to the public sector (by creating the state-held Thai Asset Management Corporation). Ultimately, the state is taking on the debt, which it will transfer through taxation to the populace, who now, in effect, owe money on goods they have not yet bought.

But while the VAT is, of course, a regressive tax, it is not as regressive as it could be, as so much of the economic activity of the poor is undocumented and takes place in street markets, in purchases from independent street vendors. One could say that the poorer you are, the less likely you are to be paying sales tax on everyday items. But that changes when lower prices for essential goods, tax included, draw you into the visible economy. Hence red carpets for the megamarts of transnational corporations that squeeze out the microcapitalized village and town markets. Hence national and transnational capital reestablish their partnership after having once gone awry, and the buck stops in an elsewhere that is nevertheless increasingly integrated into this rescheduled fold.

Similarly, there is a drive to expand the consumer credit market, with Citicorp Visa as the major player, which will further increase the documentation of consumer transactions as well as increase the business at the megamarts, which all accept Visa. Typical credit card rates are 24 percent per annum, one-third less than the godmothers' rates and way less than the godfathers' rates and, until recently, available only to those with documented income as opposed to loans offered by informal lenders, who have other means of risk management. Recently, Bankok Bank Ltd. has responded to Citicorp by allowing those with stable bank statements but without documented income to be issued a credit card. And now, following the new government's economic plan (that Thai consumers consume the nation's way out of the recession), a new reform in consumer credit law allows for the extension of consumer credit to those with undocumented income on virtually whatever terms the creditor decides. With this expansion of the reach of corporate credit into the undocumented economy, the market for out-of-the-system money is now just beginning to be encroached upon by the far lower credit rates, which the transnational credit funds can afford to extend. This may appear to be an ethically superior arrangement. In fact, it is obviously so, at least when looked at from a singularly narrow perspective, such as the interest rate charged. And yet there are various and broader contexts in which to situate the relative morality of interest rates. While Visa may be a good deal on an individual level, more broadly it increases regressive taxation and increases the integration of local economy with transnational capital funds (and like Visa Corp,

Thai banks are thoroughly integrated in terms of international investors and investments). Just as important, the expansion of legitimate corporate credit makes it increasingly more desirable for new governments to sound the call for a crackdown on illegal lending, among other illicit and "irrational" things in Thailand, which is all part of a broader atmosphere of reformism that has settled upon the country since the crash of 1997.

Darkness into the Light

The idea that Thailand is corrupt is not only a belief circulated by international investment watchdogs that rate countries on a corruption scale but a belief widely held within the country, no doubt for some good reasons. In previous decades, when the United States backed the Thai military, and so also its repressive effects on political life in the country, much of the energy in Thai national discourse was focused on political corruption in high places even if such discourse itself often had to take secret or peripheral circuits due to state and military control of mass-media capital. But since 1997, in a way not unlike the influence of the World Trade Center disaster in the United States, the financial crash in Thailand swept some of the most pressing social concerns away, suddenly, with the single-minded focus on a single issue and experience.[1] But it is not as though corruption has left the moral scene. Far from it, obviously, in a situation shot through with moral pronouncements on the rationality and virtue of economic conduct. Perhaps nothing could indicate the extent of this shift better than the transformation of one of the most popular television shows dedicated to exposing corruption that was carried on what was at the time a newly established independent network, iTV (the only nonstate television channel), a network which was created in the wake of heavy state censorship during the massacre of unarmed prodemocracy protestors in 1992 and owned by soon-to-be prime minister Thaksin Shinawatra.[2] The original gung-ho exposé-reporter's spirit of iTV had not been exorcized since the appearance of national economic trauma, however, but was channeled toward new bodies. As quickly as political corruption ceased to be a focus of attention on the show, all kinds of other corruption reappeared as iTV's flagship hidden-camera program. *Taud Rahat* ("Breaking the Code") turned its secret cameras on a different array of smaller public secrets with the most frequent coverage focused, ironically, on two particular forms: exposing the fraud of spirit mediums and exposing the operations of small-time illegal gambling. And since network television first turned its gaze to spirit mediums, local officials began efforts to curtail their activities, invoking business and medical law, and they began publicity-oriented crackdowns on gambling soon after. But more pervasive than the direct application of law enforcement was the idea of surveillance; both spirit mediums and gamblers are now in constant fear of secret cameras however statistically unlikely exposure might be. This fear was successfully harnessed in the service of the criminal/corporate finance regime in the locality of much of my fieldwork in Northern Thailand, for instance when the last known funeral casino in the area was broken up by a cell-phone call into the casino floor warning that iTV was on its way. Tables and chairs went toppling over in a stampede both like and unlike the way it used to happen when the police had not gotten their cut.

And then, with funeral casinos banned in the area — supposedly because the police are afraid of getting caught by iTV — the more secretive gambling dens that were run in connection with crime syndicates had the monopoly, providing the police with safer and more steady sources of secret income. Gambling, separated from its moral economy in exchange with the dead, from public religious observance, and from public visibility, has instead been enabling the more truly dysfunctional betting behavior of its worst victims, precisely those who are invoked as the moral justification for the elimination of this corruption of society. Similarly, the underground lottery in the region has become more centralized, protected, and bankrolled by organized crime syndicates as well (although this had already started to be the case in other regions). In the Northern Thai region of concern here, an increasing amount of underground lottery profits go directly to a well-connected figure who has some leverage over police practice and who is far beyond enforcement or reform. At this time, I would estimate that a majority of bets in this locality are ultimately backed not by independent individuals but by a hierarchical scheme that leads back to this figure. Ultimately, the profits make their way into a national political party through vote buying for local candidates, and so, in a roundabout way, make their way back again to the bettors and small-time agents. Redistribution remains the rule, as it did in less centralized and monopolized forms of undocumented speculative instruments, but, of course, this is a different and more dangerous redistribution than, say, the one between gamblers, families of the deceased, a few low-level policemen, and a host of spirit mediums as well as some monks to perform the forecasting and commentary.

The illicit valence that gambling, spirit mediumship, magic, and other "irrational" practices take on in public media is tied closely to the moral regimes that seek them out as a sign of extreme times. But against the discourse of economic reason-in-the-real, founded on a shifting frontier between legal global gaming and the morally hazardous wilds of illegal local gambling, stands a spectrum, whether seen or not, of innumerable and perhaps incommensurable financial instruments issued in idioms of spirit belief, magic, divination and prophecy, and irregular bonds funding public works through excessive, wasteful, drunken, and ecstatic exchanges that resist inspection and therefore the surrender of society to economy.

Dark finance.

Ooh, "dark finance" — uttered with the accompaniment of a fake burlesque scary gesture — a mass of "superstition" and "fetishism" that, when deliberately left unfathomable, can be pried loose from its embedded power to oppose the economic real with the socially real. In Northern Thailand, the money tree is a sovereign sign whereby value reproduces itself.[3] Strictly speaking, *money* doesn't grow on trees in Thailand, but something else that we might call, as they do, *bun*, or Buddhist merit-karma, the effect on the world produced by giving in the interest of higher communal purpose and one's own interest simultaneously. In a loose way, all monetary instruments are, in part, held to account by the moral standards embodied in the ideals that the money tree represents: life, growth, the Buddha's enlightenment, the many branches that are separate and yet connected to and emanating from a trunk, the principle that this spiritual value has the nature of increase, and the no-less-miraculous principle that the growth springs from a seed, an apparently lifeless object that contains life potential far beyond its appearance or mass. This giving establishes, expresses, and evaluates the bonds between people in the "welfare village" and the "architecture of finance" in the countryside. Its shade has extended, in some small or large part, over much of everything that happens in "dark finance," and though there are other shadows rising, it still remains the case that a large part of the "irrational" practice of money here is connected to an excessive expenditure given over to Buddhist monks, village improvement projects, and in other illegal gambling activities held at funeral rites, to families in misfortune.

All this is not to say that the complex moral economy at play under the money tree is one of undifferentiated communal sharing. Redistribution is, of course, only one process among many at work here. The conjuries of spiritual forecasting; gambling and the underground lottery; donations to monks (some with their own moral problems and failings, not to mention institutions in need of reform); and constant cycling between extensions of loans, debts, and public works all support hierarchies of the rich and the not-rich; hierarchies of those possessing spiritual authority and those who do not; and divisions between those who, on balance, prosper and those who are ruined. Most participants recognize that their local world is not an ideal world, and almost everyone involved can, if called upon, apply a moral code to the entire situation that would pointedly separate the "good" from the "bad." And increasingly in national discourse, they are being called upon to see their worlds in such a way, to make their moral vision and practical reality coincide, conform.

But the bound-yet-contradictory presences of doubtful forecasting and monetary speculation, of self-interested pursuits and essential social commerce, of gambling and complex economies of moral authority, are, of course, not unique to this provincial locale. If anything, the fact that such contradictions still manage to remain in play on this level, rather than being organized and coordinated into a consistent unity, is what remains distinctive and valuable here. By contrast, when, as in the United States, corporate scandals that erupted after the boom of the '90s, it appears that forecasting analyses, lending for speculative ventures, the offering of public companies, and accounting and regulation mechanisms have been working all along in a well-oiled collusion, that is when the alarms should go off.

And yet there is a coordination of sorts under the money tree as well, an incomplete and elusive coordination, but one that, on balance, serves the community well. All transactions find a way to be connected, if only in part, to what Georges Bataille called "the accursed share," an excessive expenditure of surplus.[4] It was in pointing to such giving, but in particular to what he called the "spirit of the gift" as an embodiment of reciprocity, that Marcel Mauss made his plea for the welfare state, arguing that "archaic" practices of gift exchange contained within them the fully human accounting of social relationships that individualized money economies could not bear out. He argued that the state must take over some of these gift-like relationships in exchange with its citizens, such as in becoming a partner in social security and welfare, thus advocating moral hazard as a rational principle. Nowadays, it is a ubiquitous practice of such states, most of which take on some sort of patron responsibility, that in order to keep up their gift-like obligations to their people, they often have to resort to gambling to generate the money. In this, state lotteries — like church bingo, funeral casinos, and black-market number rackets under money trees in Northern Thailand — are rarely allowed to be conducted without the specific earmarking of the profits for gift-like exchanges. But one difference between these and state-sponsored or other forms of gambling are the degrees of monopolization involved.

As exclusive rights to possess knowledge of economy, to sell instruments of speculation, to issue credit, and to connect social security with corporate security become increasingly coordinated and organized into stable and powerful social forms, ideologies of international finance organize in opposition to the idea of social connectedness, in opposition to patron moral hazards, arguing that the whole conduct of international finance, currency trade, and economic diagnosis and forecasting should be given free play and can operate largely without anything more than a severely atrophied sovereign sign of the gift at work. And this truth is established by gambling not simply with money but also with truth and the authority to speak truth and so, ultimately, with prophecy and morality.

But just as the implicit knowledge of economy in the Northern Thai funeral casino and the money tree recognizes that the social itself is constituted in nothing else but moral hazards, so too there is, and can be, no other structure to the global economy than moral hazard. At the moment, international governing organizations and powerful nations (each with debt far greater than the combined debt of the "corrupt" Asian states) set the rules for this regime of responsibility on their own terms, determining whom to bail out, when, and by how much. Considerable debate is waged over whether there should be any bailouts at all. They contribute to moral hazard. They allow countries to avoid facing the economic realities. But as the bailout — first, of a large transnational hedge fund and then of numerous banks and investment firms — by the United States government indicates, if the apparent results of failed risky ventures are scary enough, somebody will do something. They must. In this sense, moral hazard is always already implied. In this sense, to think that the "unnatural" creation of moral hazard within the "natural" free market is what encourages dangerous risk, as the current economic discourse assumes, is to not fully comprehend the socially embedded nature of economy. In fact, risk can, does, and will create moral hazard all on its own. The more the risk, the more likely somebody will have to do something even before institutionalized structures are in place to routinize moral hazard. Thus, in any risky situation that is not going well, the rational thing to do is to increase risk, not because there may be safety net in place for you but because only an increase in risk will ensure that one will have to be woven for you.

But, of course, although I adopt the tone of game theory here, this is not a truth that applies homogeneously to rational economic actors abstracted from social and historical context. In fact, it is not true of any individual actors at all. It is true only of the particular historical configurations of economic systems themselves. The current virtual world of financial communication is now embarking on a massive, risky venture, betting that its vision of the economic is right, wagering its stakes and prophecies through organizational structures that the rest of us have no say in, and by a moral authority it has long been distilling through its narrow conception of economy, for itself alone. But as people with more generous understandings of economics know, the return on the gift, the relations of moral hazard, are there whether we acknowledge them or not. The gamble that international finance is now taking is something we are all going to have to pay for one way or another. And the greater its risk, the more it binds us to itself.

Meanwhile, the complex of practices under the Northern Thai money tree, in their very "darkness" and invisibility, not only resist financial surveillance but, for now, still defer the desired fragmentary social relations with ulterior arrangements of hierarchy and social welfare, unsettling the conventional market with an illicit fusion of Buddhism, spirit possession, gambling, public works, and irregular financial instruments. Far from a necessarily occluded perception, dark finance can appraise the ever-present operations of moral hazard grounded within social relations even as it resists the dismantling of the social itself, but only for so long as its social viability is not undercut nor its insight into the socially real transformed by analysis into a blindness for the sake of a monopoly on prophetic insight into the true spirit of the times.

Dark finance has been singled out for suppression. Yet the only illegal economies that are vulnerable to such suppression are the small-time games and funds of the welfare village. Gambling is driven, then, into the arms of more secretive and hierarchical mafia dens, and thus the neoliberal mirror of production creates Asian cronyism to order. In this way, too, is dark economics disempowered, bringing under further control those who must now depend on highly manipulated legal structures for defense from these truly dangerous illegal entities, which grow like leaves on a money tree. What serves this "new order," then, is not only a budding illegalization of the Thai welfare state against the global ideal of a future financial order but also a trickle down of an array of discounting and dismantling mechanisms to the villages based on the illegibility and therefore illegitimacy and illegality of their irrational economics. Thus, they are to be left with nothing but the gift of reason, courtesy of the International Moral Fund, a gift of reason with which, presumably, they are supposed to survive, each to her or his own.

I HAVE TAKEN THIS HOST ONLY BECAUSE OF HIS INTERESTS, his interests in financial crashes and their reincarnation in postcrashing forms and especially in how money and spirits are at stake, but also because he never understood that this is nothing new, because I want him to see that this has all happened before just as it will continue to happen. It is always postcrashing from where I see things.

Now is not the first time we have had to fend this off, and it will not be the end of it. Of all beings, I would know, since one time when it happened, it was I, myself, in fact, who played a crucial role. But, then again, it was not really "me." As the trouble expanded, I receded, actually, and something else took my place.

This is difficult to relate, but it started with the impending demise of Ba Jae, my strongest remaining connection to this world.

As Ba Jae's fortune fell, so did her spirits. And as her spirits fell, so did mine. That first period ended, which I look back upon now as though it were like a newlywed couple before they have babies. That is a strange analogy to make about Ba Jae and me. But I felt fresh and happy, with my important job following the husbands around, consulting with Ba Jae — or that's how I imagined it — about very important matters that were her deepest secrets and concerns that no one else in the village knew.

But when Ba Jae became weak, the poisonous body came back to me. At first it was like an echo or a flash of lighting in the distance; there it was and then gone again. At first it would happen only when I was around others, never when I was alone. Around adults, mostly family, when they would ask me for the numbers.

From their perspective, I suppose they thought it was funny. I would freeze up for a split second and then blurt out a number. It was often right or very close. Enough so that my mother would begin to worry about too many people finding out. That they might start coming to the house like I was a spirit medium or some kind of divine being, and they would begin doing all kinds of strange things. Or else some of the local lottery dealers might get mad at her, refuse to take her bets, or even try to find someone who could curse us.

But I was already cursed. The poison body. It feels like you, yourself, your body, is an alien thing, attacking, noxious, and unliving, like metal, the taste of metallic shavings. The nausea began to slowly creep back into my life, like I wanted to throw up my whole body from the inside. Eventually it would visit me at night when I tried to sleep.

And it didn't come alone.

Sometimes I would be up all night with the feeling there was someone, a man, standing next to my bed. I couldn't see it but almost sort of feel him there, and there was some kind of deep, seeping anger about to set upon me. Other times, it was like there was a black cloud pressing down on me, and I couldn't breathe. I would become terrified, but I couldn't move or scream and would think that if I couldn't breathe, no one would know, and no one could help me. Often I would have to suffer through this all night, paralyzed but fully awake, alone, hour after hour.

Sometimes, if people were up late at night, partying at a funeral casino, the music would start to really annoy me. I found it unbearable, the screeching, xylophonic cascades and whining clarinets. And then it would go from sounding like crying, which it was supposed to, to sounding like speaking, which was not supposed to happen. Late at night I would start to feel the poison body and the unbearable screeching, and I would hear voices in the music, whispering to me in the dark.

I couldn't tell what they were saying and did not want to know. I would try to take my mind away from it, looking up out of my window at the moon.

The moon, dear moon. In all these years it has been my one and only friend, my only peace in this life and the next.

One of my other favorite things in all the world did not prove as trustworthy. And that was going to see the movies. In those days we only had movies in the temple or at someone's house if they had a big enough field behind it. A movie projector, movie, and sound system were things you could rent as an investment and charge people to come watch. One of my uncles was the sound man for foreign movies (which most movies were) from America and India or sometimes Hong Kong. He was a great impersonator of men's and women's voices, and although he could not read or write and could barely speak Central Thai let alone another foreign language, he could tell what the story was about just from watching and was able to put it into our Northern Thai, *kam muang* words. He almost never stammered or interrupted the flow of things in any way. The voices just poured out of him. He was really into it, and so were we all, and rarely were we thrust out of the world he wrapped us into.

But occasionally the interpretation would be so ridiculous in relation to the picture. Or he would slip in some kind of reference to village affairs, such as something about the manner in which a specific young lad was courting a young woman with inadequate gifts and without bathing himself first, and then everyone would laugh and come out of the spell.

But, for me, I got pulled out of the spell in a completely different way. It was my curse: it began to take away the one thing that used to be so easy to escape into. It started one night when the thought crossed my mind that there were not a lot of people in the audience.

They were all short of cash. It was another reminder of the weakness spreading.

I was listening to the voice-over on the PA system for a movie about a gang or something, and the mafia boss, an Englishman with a sick laugh and eyes crazed with greed, was planning some vicious kung fu murder of the Chinese hero. All the money and girls would then be his. And as he threatened to make this man die by tearing up his body, I had the overwhelming feeling that the Englishman was speaking directly to me. He was talking out of the movie and directly to me, threatening me with the violent acts he was cooking up in his demented mind.

After that, even when passing by a radio or hearing films broadcast from some nearby location, in the day or night, the voices would often be speaking directly to me. Whatever they said applied specifically to me. There were no stories for me anymore. I hated stories and did not want to go near them.

And then, even if I did not go near them, there was still music. It didn't have to be funeral casinos anymore. Often I would hear voices and whispers in music, anything that came out of a loudspeaker, a phonograph, a radio, had messages in it speaking directly to me. So I could not go near these things, and that made my family and my mother very worried about my strange behavior. I rarely ventured into the heart of our village, where people tended to have radios and such. It was like everything to do with communication was spitting me out of itself.

That's why I would take to the trees. For a short time I actually became a good student because I would spend my free days and free time up in trees, where it was calm and quiet and no voices could get to me. There were trees with giant branches and thick leaves where I could lie out and take a nap if I wanted. I would get books, my meal, my water, my dessert that my mother would make for me, and I would have everything I needed, and no one could find me, and I could be up there without interruption and without voices. And as I ate my sweets up there, safe in my tree, I could feel my mother's love in every taste.

Well that lasted for a time. Eventually I would have to pee, and so I would just hold on to a branch and squat down and pee.

But one time when I did this, I began to hear voices again. A man's voice, loud, cursing and swearing, threatening to kill me.

It turned out to be a real voice. It was Iy Noon, I realized, and he was furious that someone had peed on him, yelling, "Who is it? Who is it? Who is it up there?" So I just stayed still, and he could not see me, and I could not see him, and he was too fat to climb the tree, so he eventually went away.

Another time the opposite happened. Iy Lucky, a local funeral casino dealer, came to my tree to take a piss, and I saw him. I saw his ugly penis and his yellow pee. He had no idea I was there.

Eventually it would get cold, my mother would be worried, and I would have to come down. And that was often the time of day when people would listen to radios or play music, so I had to walk really fast all the way home and try to ignore the whispering. I wouldn't tell anyone about it, though, because I had the idea that if they found out, they would do terrible things to me like drill into my head or send me away.

Instead I clung to my duties as a spy. A secret spy with a secret mission. I was chosen above all others by Ba Jae for this. Only me. And only we knew about it, no one else. It was so secret that sometimes Ba Jae would act like she did not know me. Perhaps she did that, I thought, because she knew when there might be other presences there, listening to our minds.

And, as a spy, I had something to take my mind off everything that was pressing against me. Far better to watch others than to witness what was happening to myself.

7:00 AM   Number One wakes up and heads out to do make a number two. Or so I guess. Actually, this morning I am not there to witness the morning miracle, but I am waiting far ahead, far down the road to the pool hall, which is not open at this hour and toward which he has been pedaling his bicycle every morning for no apparent reason. It is the first day after my great discovery of the case of money from town. I had reported it to Ba Jae, but that did not diminish her insistence that I watch the other husbands.

I am waiting far ahead on the road out to the middle of nowhere, and see Number One come and pass right under the tree I am hiding in. Suddenly, with a quick glance over the shoulder, he dips off the road and coasts, bumping and shaking over hard patches of weed, and plunges into the forest edge.

I leap down from the tree and follow, stepping into the forest where he entered. It is thick forest. I am startled at how suddenly the bright morning sunlight has become as if dusk. I begin to walk through the brush, listening for Number One's sounds, which are abrupt, crashing this way and that. But despite how loud he is, it takes a while to locate him. I keep getting distracted by the feeling of bugs or worms crawling over my body. When I pause to brush them off, there is nothing there. I even feel some kind of bug fly in my ear and wiggle around in it, but again, nothing there. And the farther I walk, the darker it gets.

During those times, my fear of stories, of movies, of music, started to take a strange turn. Soon I started to get really confused. It started to become normal that voices in the films and stories were talking directly to me. So it was not fear anymore but like a strange feeling I could not bear. Soon it felt like regular life, especially when I would come down from the trees and be around people, like what was happening with and around them and me was not real. Like real life was the story and I was a part of it. Like I was not real. Like I was just a figment of imagination, part of something bigger, beyond my skin and my body. So sometimes I would look my mother in the eye, and for a second it felt like she could read my thoughts. When I would write something down in my notebook for school, I could feel the notebook sitting there in our living room, and it felt like *they* could read it. Whenever I would write things down in it, they would know. They would know what I was reading for school when I would read it, like the voice in my head was their voice in their head. And I didn't even know who *they* were. If I had bad thoughts about people, they would know. It wasn't even that I was trying to keep people safe anymore, it was like I was fighting to keep my own self, my own thoughts, to myself.

And then they started to comment. They started to talk back.

When I would tell them to shut up, they would only talk louder and say mean things to me.

Other times, I couldn't tell whether I said something out loud or not. I would think that I said something, but when I checked with other people around me, they had heard nothing.

I didn't feel like my body was my body or my self was my self. It was like I wasn't living life from my point of view. The whole world began to seem like a dream or some story that I was just a tiny part of, no more important than any of the rest. Or I would feel as though I were no longer part of the physical world, as though I were no longer bound by the barrier of my skin, that nothing was real and what was in me was also outside of me and what was outside of me was also in me and it was all part of something else. And it felt like the source of all this trouble wasn't coming from me; it was coming from everyone else, from all of them.

Sometimes my mother would come look for me and try to get me to come down from the tree, and I wouldn't want to come down and face all their weirdness.

❧ I stepped through the forest, following him, and it got darker and darker the closer and closer I got to his crashing, thrashing sounds. Suddenly I arrived at a tiny clearing where large *takien* branches from several trees formed an open arch over a somewhat rocky patch. And there was Number One, now with a shovel in hand and a pick lodged in the dirt beside him. He was digging with a crazed look in his eyes, sweat pouring over him. It was at that moment that I noticed for the very first time something that should have been obvious: that he was a frail, weak, pale man, and I was overcome by the conviction that he was, in fact, dying. I even imagined for a moment that I could smell his death.

I watched him secretly for a time from behind a screen of brush until, by accident, I shifted my foot and brushed against a large, dry, hard teak tree leaf that made a scraping sound over the ground. Number One stood up with a jerk, beads of sweat whipping off his body. His look went straight to the pickax, and so did mine. But then he just threw down his shovel and squatted low to the ground, eyes darting back and forth.

I was still. He was still. We were like one mind, both incredibly vigilant and quiet. Everything extra in the world being burned up in the furnace of our attention, our single-minded focus on not being detected.

Finally, after an endless and timeless span, he stood up again. I remained more motionless than ever. He picked up his shovel, and in the very next dig he hit on something, fell to his knees, out of my sight, and when he emerged, he had a twisted grin as he began furiously tugging away at something.

He was carrying something heavy, something stiff, a body, a human body wrapped with blessing string around the ankles and wrists, the body of a man, partly decomposed, but not so far eaten by worms and bugs that I could not see that it was Gongkam, my uncle Gongkam.

❧ "Let me tell you something," Ba Jae said after sitting me down in the only moment when she revealed not only some of what was going on around her but also the true meaning of it all. "Make no mistake, there is no limit to their hunger. It is blind, unfeeling. Do not be fooled by their human faces. Their human expressions. There is nothing human about them. They are not like you and me. They are not *of* us. They are simply *among* us. They want more and more and more, and this is something that they cannot change, cannot control, cannot make to increase or decrease but is an infinite desire without end. They are ghosts! There is no way they will be stopped, unless *we* stop them. And we cannot stop them."

We had been speaking of the mafia, who were like ghosts closing in on her, and of Husbands Numbers One and Two, and Ba Jae confessed to me that her plans were crumbling around her. She had intended to build a super marketplace with fancy row houses with shop fronts, all made from cement. They would have been the center of commerce in the area. Everyone would have bought and sold there. It would all have been aboveboard. She had the land. She had the money.

And then it all started slipping away. The godfathers came in. They wanted the loan market. They wanted the land. They wanted her out.

"We cannot stop them alone. We need help. And you, you, Anchalee, you will bring us our help."

Seeing the decomposed face of my uncle Gongkam, I was suddenly shocked back into my body for an instant, where I found that I, too, was sweating. I was panting, and I could not control it. But Husband Number One was so enraptured by his find that he didn't notice me. He grabbed the pickax. He held its pointed edge close to Gongkam's face. He gripped it as if taking aim. He raised it over Gongkam's head and then let it fall upon his forehead with a sickening *thwack*, a surprisingly soft cracking sound that shuddered through my body, violently and suddenly.

I was dizzy, unbalanced. And then it rose in me. The poisonous body, the metallic body. So fast and strong, so suddenly, that in little more than one instant, everything went black.

9 · THE RETURN OF THE DEAD

THE ROOT OF A TREE.

The bark wrinkled and cracked.

Cold yellow wax seeped into the crevices.

Half-burned candles.

Dried-out old flowers, dusty ribbons, and a pile of sacred sticks propped on the trunk.

I look up the trunk and then at something pulsing in the leaves.

A white branch.

My vision is fuzzy. When I look down to focus, I see him, Number One, squatting, sweaty, looking into the dirt while wiping his brow with a cloth. Suddenly I remember what he did, striking through the skull of Gongkam with a pickax, and my guts are filled with dread, sinking weight.

I realize am in the last place I would ever have expected to be, at her tree. I try, but I can't move my body, and then he sees me.

"You were not supposed to see that," he said grimly. There is nothing special in his eyes. I wrench my body around, wondering whether I am tied up.

I am not. Motion begins to come back to my body a bit.

"She said that now it is time for you to know."

A million thoughts pass by at a time like this. What are they doing, and what are they going to do to me? Who is "she," and what does she want me to know?

I manage to sit up, and I don't know what to be more afraid of, him or the tree. I start to scoot back inch by inch.

"Don't do that. She said I was to stay with you."

Number One stands up. I see again the dying man I saw before.

"Look, she told me to do it. She told me to dig up Gongkam and split his skull. It was the only way. She told me to follow her here. I have to do what she says, right? And so do you."

"I *want to*, I want to do what she says." It just comes out of my mouth. My jaw and lips move as if I am a puppet. It feels and sounds like someone else's voice is creaking out of my throat. "And I'm going to tell Ba Jae everything."

And no sooner do I say that than footsteps begin to fall on the hard, dry teak leaves, and Ba Jae comes into the clearing, her head darting this way and that.

"I got here as fast as I could," she blurts out to Number One, and then she looks down on me.

"Jae, she saw everything, and then the jow came and took her and commanded me to come to her here. She told me to bury Gongkam somewhere around here, where no one will know."

"OK, then, do it," Ba Jae says coldly to him, but then a flash of something appears in her eyes. Pity? "I knew I could trust you." Then she looks down at me. "I will take care of the girl."

I feel weak again and unable to concentrate on the details of things they are saying to each other, speaking without hardly a glance to me, and as though I am not really here. I just know that I am in for something terrible tonight.

I don't know whether you know fear in the night. Real night, not like the night of these days, lit up by electricity or heat or air or television at your beck and call. A real, black night when unnaturally cold winds penetrate the cracks in your walls, a storm coming, with flashes of light, sometimes followed by silence, sometimes by a loud crack, sound that has shaken you and dug itself deep down into your chest and into your heart ever since you were a baby and before.

That night Iy Lert was playing cards with Iy Sert and Iy Noon, but they had fallen to sleep in a drunken stupor. They didn't go out to find a funeral casino as they normally would but had stayed in drinking. It was a dark night. Dogs barked in the distance. And Iy Lert was left in the flickering candlelight, alone in his own drunken stupor and a little nervous what with the barking and the dark, and so he was flipping the cards, one by one, taking his mind off everything by trying to guess what they would be. He was half-mindedly doing it, taking a card off the top of the deck, thinking, *ace of diamonds*, flipping it over with a toss before him, and so on.

The cold wind seeped through the wall boards and touched the back of his neck. He thought to himself, *jack of clubs*, and flip . . . there it was!

"Whoh! Look!" he stammered, swinging his head up like it weighed fifty kilos and was hard to stop. "Look, you guys, I did it!" But they just lay dead still, no sounds but the dogs barking and Iy Noon snoring like a tiger.

He thought, *five of diamonds*, and flip, there it was!

Ace of spades. Again. He went faster and faster. *Four of hearts.* Again. *Ten of clubs.* And flip . . . there it was.

Gurgling stammers of "Whoh." "Hit it." "Victory." Even his laughter was garbled. But not his predictions.

He sat up, eyes greedy, wide, and he flipped over card after card, every one exactly what he expected.

And not a soul around to see it, or, for that matter, to accept a wager on it.

No one. But on the windowsill, a sparrow, cocking its head this way and that at him. *Three times.* Geckos on the ceiling. *One, two, three, four* of them.

Five of hearts. Hit it. *Seven of diamonds.* Hit it. *Two of spades . . .*

He was going so fast now he didn't even have time to try to think of a card, but the thought would just pop up in his mind on its own. He started flipping and tossing the cards as fast as he could, and he could hear it, *five of diamonds, ten of clubs, king of spades . . .*

The sparrow on his windowsill was cocking its head this way and that. *One, two, three, four* times.

Seven of hearts, three of diamonds, five of clubs . . . the voice went on and on, and then he realized . . .

It was not his voice.

Eight of hearts, three of hearts, eight of clubs, jack of spades . . .

It was Gongkam. The dead man had gotten into his head.

Iy Lert yelped and threw down the cards, backpedaled with his hands while kicking away the cards like they were poisonous spiders. *One, two, three, four, five* kicks.

He screamed a second time. *Two* screams, and whirled around and ran *one, two, three, four, five, six, seven* steps for the doorway, Gongkam's voice counting along the way, getting louder, and Iy Lert passed the sparrow cocking its head *one, two, three* times and he went *one, two, three, four, five, six, seven, eight, nine, ten* down the stairs and ran past *one, two, three, four, five* houses and *one, two, three* people saw him. *One* spoke *four* words to him, "Hey, where you going?" And the other *two* spoke *seven* words to him each, "What is wrong with you Iy Lert?" and "Don't you know there is a funeral tonight?"

It was all Gongkam's voice, counting in his head. With dead calm, even, quick, but louder and louder, clearer and clearer.

Iy Lert cupped both hands over his ears, really pressing hard, yelling, "Shut up, shut up, shut up," and every time he told Gongkam to shut up, the voice counted in his head. *One. Two. Three.*

After an uncountable amount of time stumbling around the village in chaos, confusion, and terror at the growing voice of numbers in his head, he eventually walked, by random chance, into the temple, where he hastily blurted out a stream of babble, mostly numbers, to the old abbot, who told him to calm down, and Iy Lert just answered him back with more numbers. The monks led Iy Lert into the chapel while Old Man Moom, the monks' attendant in the temple, trailed behind, desperately trying to write down all the numbers coming out of Iy Lert's mouth. Some monks were there in the chapel to chant while the abbot tied Iy Lert's wrists together with sacred twine and also tied it around his forehead and then sprinkled him with holy water on top of that.

Finally, Iy Lert began to calm down, and the numbers turned into words, and he explained what had happened.

But by that time the whole village was abuzz. People were running this way and that, screaming about all kinds of things they had seen here and there, all over the place.

But it was all really about one thing. Gongkam had come back. He was back for more dead to keep him company.

❧ The wind of an approaching storm. A feeling of things out of joint, un-naturally cool, of suspended temperature, of suspended time. And the feeling in the dark, even if you cannot see what it is, of something out there, something large, very, very large, pressing, insistent, inescapable, inevitable.

Every few minutes a flash of distant lightning would vaguely light up the village, and everyone would see each other, huddled here or there or running around with frightened faces. Dogs were barking everywhere, including from far out, deep in the fields, where they kept guard over the few men who were working so hard that they slept in the fields, where it was cool.

Stories shouted out over the confusion. Several families had seen the exact same thing in their different houses. Exactly the same thing.

It was Gongkam in the kitchen. He was squatting down and dipping his finger into one of their empty pots and licking it. His face all white, eyes black, and his mouth red. His dirty teeth bared from behind a grin. When he was discovered there, he looked up from the pot with a finger in his mouth and with a hungry look that took all the strength out of your legs, and you can't find your breath.

And he was very present at one house in particular, that of his sister, Ee Nieo, the stingy groceries merchant who was also one of several local dealers in black-market lottery. She was one of the most popular ones to place a bet with because she was considered a lucky choice even though her prosperous operation meant that this could not possibly be the case. And her family was in more terror and confusion than any other because they said they looked and looked, and they could not find Ee Nieo any-where. She had been sleeping on her mat when Gongkam came, and now she was gone.

The headman and several of the older men were, however, becoming more level-headed and eventually organized half the village to parade through the lanes, bearing kerosene lanterns, beating drums and pans, lighting firecrackers to scare away the ghost.

Meanwhile, one of the younger monks, a *maha* who had studied scrip-ture in Bangkok for a few years, was having none of this and got someone to take him around atop a pickup truck with the temple's PA system on board, hooked up to a noisy gas generator, and he countered their pro-cession with his own extremely noisy but barely comprehensible auditory spectacle, exhorting everyone to put down their weapons, to abandon their unmodern un-Buddhist superstitions and emerge out of darkness and fear.

This, of course, could provide no consolation for the family of Ee Nieo, whose mother, husband, two daughters, and one son-in-law were up at the front of the line of the antighost parade, the whole line of which was now in no mood to even take any prisoners. When they eventually came head-to-head with the monk's pickup, it had to come to a halt, and they formed two columns and passed him by, slapping the sides and yelling at him to go back to the temple, that they would handle this.

Then the storm hit, shattering thunder and sheets of rain slapping down on everyone, most of whom then proceeded to run feverishly to the temple for cover, where they might be safe from the ghost and could stay together. The abbot and many of the monks stayed with them, chanting, and things calmed down until they discovered Iy Lert there, whom the abbot was trying to hide in order to avoid more chaos, and they learned from him yet another terrible story of Gongkam's visit in the night.

Almost immediately, after stammering out his story, Iy Lert's face went white as he gaped at one of the bote's many windows. Everyone whipped their heads around and then began screaming, "Gongkam, Gongkam," and the children were crying and the old women clutching them and each other while others pressed their palms together, shut their eyelids tight, and chanted to themselves as loudly as would drown out the din around them but no louder.

Many people said they had seen Gongkam in the window, looking in, with his black eyes and pale face, baring his dirty teeth, and licking his finger with a very, very long red tongue.

இ Halfway through the night, after the storm passed and some people were able to fall asleep in a pile, word came in of the missing woman. It was Iy Sert and Iy Noon who came bounding into the temple, looking for everyone and waking everyone up again. They were still drunk, talking loudly and nervously over each other, sometimes saying the exact same thing as they blurted out their story. Apparently, they had slept through most of the commotion and had woken up only an hour before. They found the cards scattered everywhere and no sign of Iy Lert and thought something terrible had happened and so set out looking for him, following the sounds of dogs barking out in the fields.

The rain had just stopped, and everything was muddy, but they stepped carefully about a hundred meters down the red-dirt path leading to the fields that fronted the creek. They braced themselves, walking like that out into the dark with the dogs barking. Then they saw something ahead, squatting in the road. It looked like a giant white cat hunched over something.

But when they got closer, they could see it was a human-like figure. They were terrified but also feared for Iy Lert. Maybe it was him, gone mad drunk or something. So they pressed on, carefully putting down each step along the way so that they would not slip in the mud. And their feet became heavy with mud, with mud sticking to mud, and then they began to wonder whether they would get stuck out there in the dark. They imagined their lantern running out of kerosene or blowing out and being stuck out in the mud, in the dark, alone with it, with that.

But they got themselves free and were able to draw closer. That is when they could make it out clearly, could see it dipping its finger in something and licking it. They kept creeping closer, as if their heavy feet were being carried by the mud itself, impelled by it to take one and then another step. Closer and closer to it until it stopped dipping and licking, just stopped, still, looking down. Did it sense they were near? And then its head moved, only the head, turning slowly, evenly, to face them and bare its dirty teeth with a sick grin and red, soaked lips.

❧ What followed was the confusing part of Iy Lert and Iy Noon's story, which they stuck to yet also admitted was very strange and unlikely: when the head turned to them, they could see it was Gongkam, and they scrambled backward in fright, but almost as soon as they tried to turn and run, they stumbled over something and fell in the mud, and their faces were right in what they thought at first was a puddle of muddy water. But as everyone but them could see, they were drenched in blood.

They had stumbled over a dead body, which was not there before. They felt it in the dark. Felt warm, muddy water. They shivered and screamed. When they looked back to where they saw that thing, Gongkam, dipping its finger in something, it was gone, and gone also was whatever he had there with him, as though there had never been anything there. They ran all the way back to the village.

In the morning everyone went out to confirm their story, and that is where they found the missing woman, Ee Nieo.

After everything that happened, Ee Nieo was the only victim on that night, the night that brother Gongkam came back.

Dead from a gunshot to the back of her head. Very deliberately placed.

‡ In the morning the headman and other villagers came to see the monk Maha Paan, sorry for their harshness the night before, which was a totally inappropriate way to treat a monk, and they brought him gifts of very nice food, lotus flowers, factory-rolled cigarettes, betel nut, and more than 100 baht in cash and coin.

The police also came in the morning, out from the local outpost, to inspect the body and do an investigation, but they seemed so obviously unenthusiastic about it that it made everyone afraid, for it meant that someone very influential had almost certainly paid the officers off to look the other way. Either that or the police themselves had done it.

"REMEMBER," SHE TOLD ME, "THEY ARE GHOSTS." No limit to their hunger, blind, unfeeling. Fooling us with their human faces. But they are ghosts . . . no way they will be stopped, unless we stop them ourselves. And we cannot stop them.

A hungry ghost is obsessional, and powerless in the sense that they cannot help what they do, cannot do it more and cannot do it less. Insatiable. In fact, a hungry ghost in this sense is more human than human, the embodiment of desire in its mindless drive. Being brushed by the touch of a ghost is like being contacted by a truth of ourselves, that we were always already haunted, always already beside ourselves with want.

What could I do to stop them?

"It isn't you, little girl," Ba Jae told me. "It's *her*. If you want your problems to stop you have to accept her. And if you accept her, and do her bidding, then you will not only help yourself but help all of us as well."

And there was little time. They were coming that night. Or that was what they had threatened to do. After discovering that Number Two was in with the godfathers, that they were funneling money to the trio of lucky gamblers, Ba Jae had thrown him out. And he was furious, calling her an old hag who would soon be dead. A dead old greedy old Chinese old hag.

"What do you mean by dead?" Ba Jae demanded, unphased.

He told her that it was far past the time to give up her plans and accept that the godfathers were to handle loans now and they were going to handle the lottery as well. That you greedy Chinese should just go home and that there was going to be a message for her that night.

I felt bad to hear that because Ba Jae was half-Chinese, and she didn't seem to be greedier than any other money lender, and also I was afraid of what the message might be.

Number Two disappeared from the village after the tirade.

"The spirit of the tree has got ahold of you already, so what is the point of fighting it? She has already told us so much. That we must build her a spirit house. That we must hide Gongkam's body where the others will never find it. That Gongkam will end the winning streak and that Iy Lert's gang will experience misfortune and that I cannot go back to the village tonight. That she will protect me from them. But you have to accept her, or they will win out, own everything, and we will all be poor."

I believed Ba Jae that day. What with everything that had been happening, why would I not believe that a spirit could throw the godfathers out of our village and make us all well again? There was nothing happening in my world that did not make that seem possible. I believed her, and this is one reason I have become what I am now.

"I have been feeding her all this time, and she is pleased with me. And with you."

Number One was building a fire while we talked and had food with him, had a tarp, mats, blankets. I was dizzy with fear because it looked like they intended us to spend the night there. I thought of my mother. How she would not want me to be there. How she would never want me to accept a jow. We weren't really that type of people. Not that our family did not believe in luck and spirits and place and rituals and everything. My mother was, as you know, a consummate interpreter of omens. And yet, although we were all steeped in it, we were also an extremely practical people who did not want to get caught up in these things either. We were happy to benefit in our ordinary lives, but the ordinary life was where, without doubt, we lived, and wanted to live out, our lives.

"Your mother thinks you are staying the night at my house. But we have to head out to Baan Maitri."

At least I was relieved that we were not going to stay out in the forest.

Ba Jae looked up into the branches of the tree. "It is not safe for us in our village."

By which I think she meant *she* was not safe. Where would I be safe?

But although I was wavering, I believed her, which, as I said, is a big reason that I have become what I am today.

That night we walked to a remote village where Number One had some relatives and were greeted rather coldly but were provided with a corner in a house in which to sleep. The roof leaked. The next day, around noon, we had made our way back to Baan Sala. The sun had come out and dried out our weary, wet spirits as we entered the village, which was drenched in stories still swirling about, stories that we were soon swept up in.

Ghosts did not shoot guns. That inescapable fact threw everything into more confusion than it already was in. Where had Iy Lert gone after Iy Sert and Iy Noon fell asleep? People saw him stumbling around the village acting very strange. Had Iy Sert and Iy Noon really slept through all those drums, pans, and firecrackers? Did they really see Gongkam in the dark? And how did they really get all bloody? Were the firecrackers used as cover to hide the gunshot? Was the headman in on it? Did Ee Nieo's family kill her? What connection did Gongkam have to the death because, although he did not pull the trigger, few could doubt that he was behind the death. Did Gongkam make the killers do it to her, whoever they were? Or had he really come at all?

You can imagine all the permutations and combinations and possibilities. And those included us, of course: Where had Ba Jae and Number One been all night? And what was I doing with them?

There had been suspicion around me for some time, but it never quite all came together until that night. I was the strangest girl in the village. Always walking quickly though the street, not looking right or left, avoiding people. Other times sneaking around or disappearing into the forest and the trees, gone all day long. The strange vacant looks on my face. Rumors that I could get lottery numbers and stories that I had been possessed.

It wasn't long, maybe a few days, before I started to become the center of it all. People began to say that I was a *phii bob*. At night I would leave my body and eat the entrails of the living as they slept. They had merely seen this in the movies that they had been watching, according to my mother, who would yell at them down in the streets (that is how I heard about it; they would never say it to my face).

But people were desperate and afraid. I was simply something solid on which to pin the empty, weak sickness that was spreading through the village. Money had dried up. Outsiders had everyone in debt and were getting the land as well. Spirits were attacking. And now a woman was shot in the back of the head, killed out in the fields, which no one wanted to go out into anymore, and the rice out that way would be left unharvested, breeding first rats and then snakes.

But the worst of it, the worst of it all, was when they found out that Ee Nieo had been pregnant when she was shot. Her husband was scared out of his wits and had immediately been ordained as a monk, staying first at our temple but then so afraid that he had to transfer to another far away in Lampang Town, where there was electricity.

First Gongkam had come back. And now his sister would almost certainly be back as well. And what could be worse than a greedy pregnant woman who had been violently murdered out in the fields? There was almost nothing in the imagination that could be more double, triple, quadruple haunted than that.

When people found out about the pregnancy, all her possessions were taken from the house and broken into pieces and burned. Her bed, her mirrors, her makeup and clothes. Everything portable was taken or stripped out of the house, and the house itself was left vacant, its timbers and boards left there to the dust and weeds until many, many years later when the value of the teak wood became just too tempting.

After the police left and had what they needed for their report, Ee Nieo herself was, like her brother, taken out into the forest for a hasty burial, tied at the wrists and feet. A nail was driven into her forehead to keep the spirit trapped inside the skull, a skull that is itself trapped under the earth, under the cover of forest, out among the trees and far from the village and the land of the living.

That was the attitude at the time: that there was nothing to be done about this waste and misfortune, this twisted outcome to the birth of life, nothing but to put it out of sight and mind, where at least you could suppress it, bury it, expel it for a time, perhaps a long time, and leave it out there for others to deal with, maybe years and years later when perhaps you have already passed on to heaven and when it could no longer come back to get you.

And how many other times had this been done? How many others were out there in the forest from years and years and centuries ago, long forgotten, and whose bonds could no longer tie them, who had surfaced from the earth and taken their place among the trees, waiting for someone to wander by?

So, you see, it was the darkest time in the village, with fear of every direction. Although people had to be afraid of who might be shot next, there was still Gongkam to fear, and now Ee Nieo, and now the very strangest girl — myself — as well.

ॐ It was at this point that my mother had a change of heart. That she agreed to go along with my new spirit career. She was afraid for me. It didn't seem quite possible, yet she was nevertheless afraid that someone might go too far and even try to kill me. People were so full of fear and getting crazy all the time. Maybe she was even afraid *of* me. No one was unaware of how strange I was. She agreed to let Ba Jae take me to the spirit mediums. All the signs were there. I had been called, and that was a far more appealing explanation than that I was flying about the village at night killing people. There would be no way to rid me of my problems and no hope for the village and this sickness that had brought us all to the breaking point if I did not go along this version of events.

Of course, it would also have to be my choice. I would have to willingly give myself to the tree, whatever "willing" means in such a situation. I would have to give my body and my life over to the spirit world.

11 · DETERRITORY

WHERE DID I GO, WHEN SHE CAME?

I can understand your confusion. I am aware, of course, from perusing the memories of my host, of the science-fiction stories of downloaded personalities and so forth extracting themselves from bodies, switching bodies, leaving and entering. I am also aware of the opposite, of how some of you freeze your bodies after you are already dead, hoping for the time when your disease can be cured, thinking that your bodies are what you are. I understand how it seems that first there is something called matter, and then there is consciousness that comes from it. You feel like you are in your bodies, or you feel that you are your bodies. I have to confess that all these possibilities are very amusing to me, charming to me. If I were you, I suppose that I would try to imagine it these ways too.

While I was among the Thai, we, too, talked of bodies that spirits "take hold of" and "enter." This should not be confused with an actual description of how the process unfolds. Spirits entering bodies is what it looks like from the outside. That appearance begins with an assumption, a largely unquestioned assumption that I have found in most humans I have met, so please excuse me for being presumptuous. It is the assumption that what I am is a thing inside this body, looking out through it at a world that is out there, which is not me. In other words, there is a dividing line in reality between everything that consists of this substance you call "matter," which is on the outside and is what my body is, and an interiority, which I experience as inside this body and therefore separated also from the world of matter out there. You may call this interiority "consciousness" or something else, or pretend you don't know what I mean, or pretend that you are "nondualist" and you only believe in matter, but whatever is the case with that, it seems like it is of a different order, on the inside. With that assumption lodged in place, I totally get it why it does appear to be spirits entering and leaving these bodies/matter containers.

But this question, of where did I go when she came, is precisely the one that troubles this belief that what you are is something in a material body, for it certainly appeared that she had taken my body, but if that were the case, then where am I? And when I came back, where did I come from?

You might try, as my host has, to think of this instead in sophisticated terms of territory. As Deleuze and Guattari explain it in the books my host has read, territory is the range or field that is inhabited by patterns of activity that establish a kind of area that is not objectively located or rooted to land or even space but nevertheless exists in areas and spaces through the interrelation and interaction of individuals and groups, such as the relations between wolves in a pack or the travels of herders or nomads. They have territory in relation to other groups as well as other objects and environments. Similarly, you establish territory, for instance, on a bus by repeatedly moving your elbows onto the armrest that you never quite share with your neighbor, by how you inhabit space within a house, a working environment, or even within your own body. Territory is constantly relational, in motion and flux, and that includes the space within the body or even in the mind. It is not a given that one always inhabits the body in the same way as others or the same way as yourself in different moments and contexts. Nor is it a given that "you" simply inhabit your body; instead, "you" share your body, just like an armrest, with several other forces, emotions, thoughts, perceptions, vibrations, intensities, attractions, and repulsions. Which one is the real you? Which one has permanent right and title to this armrest, or is it instead relational? For Deleuze, "you" are just like a pack of wolves, roaming through the body and through states of mind, "dividuals" that roam not only your body and mind but others' too, including the bodies of buildings and other objects. Or even more subtly still, Guattari shows, the psychological place in which one dwells can also be said to be a territory from which one ventures forth, returns, or from which one acts, a nonfirmament, a nonsettled place, which nevertheless is inhabited.

At one point in Deleuze and Guattari, we get, of course, what I have come to expect from the French theorists I encounter in my host's memories: the expectable French typecasting of the spontaneous masochist or else madman or else artist or, better yet, masochistic mad artist serving as the exemplar of one who has passed beyond territorialization and inhabits the resistant force of deterritorialization (such a resistant force ceases as soon as the masochist feels compelled by customs, rules, or order to reperform his activities, i.e., has ceased to be avant-garde).

What is absolute deterritorialization? Is it truly to be found in an unbound masochism, in drug use, hypochondria, schizophrenia, to name a few examples explored by Deleuze and Guattari (also a notably ignorant, Orientalist take on Taoist sex alchemy), albeit with what is, for a French avant-garde, an uncharacteristic note of caution? Or is absolute deterritorialization to be found only in what can, according to Deleuze and Guattari, be properly termed "philosophy"? By contrast, is unfreedom really caused by the rule, the norm, the order, or is there a freedom that is so free it can exist within rule, order, norm (where most of us have to dwell, after all), so free that it cannot be threatened by such gross things of the "molar" level (the obvious level of conventional social scientific analysis of institutions, structures, and individuals) and can possibly even thrive within them? What sort of a groundlessness, deterritorialization, would that be?

Could it be possible that a widely cited duo of French theorists would be incapable of imagining the possibility of a real and absolute deterritorialization and that others, perhaps from other parts of the world, other times, can not only imagine it but realize it?

I wouldn't know, being that I am a mere spirit in this form, and it wasn't me who actually read this stuff.

But I can ask this: Where do I go when she comes into my body?

Let me start by putting it this way (and I will come back around to this again, for after all, this is also where my story ends): imagine you are sitting in a movie theater, and the projector is running behind you, casting light. But if there were no screen in front of you, but just a vast empty space extending into infinity, would you see the light? Is the light there when it does not fall upon anything? Mind you, there is not even a speck of dust for it to touch.

No, even though the projector is running, casting light, there is not the slightest trace anywhere of this light. But can you say it does not exist? If a speck of dust floats by somewhere in the space in front of you, then the light hits it, and it seems that it was there all along, there was light all along. But what can it mean for light to "exist" if it does not alight upon anything?

Or the question is this: What does it mean to exist as a potential that is always there, but also not really there, completely without form, boundary, substance, that one cannot see, hear, smell, touch, taste, or conceive? One cannot say that such a "thing" exists, either, or that it is a thing.

When you feel anger, the light hits upon anger, and it appears and seems as though you are feeling something and therefore that you are here. If you think of a tree, or if you smell an apple, or you touch water, or you plan your day, then, again, there are objects because light falls upon something, a sensory object or idea appears, and therefore it appears as though light is something, you are something, and then it seems as though you are here. Without light, there would be no objects: they could not appear. But without objects, there would be no way to know that there is light. And yet even in the absence of any objects, the light is there, or at least is not *not* there, because at any moment, as soon as an object arises, it will be apparent that there is light, and so the mind exists, at least as a potential that can appear at any time.

When she comes, there is no speck of dust.

This is not so easy, but it is helped along quite a lot by the fact that she is grabbing on to the dust in my stead, latching on to things stronger, harder, with a will to become, and one far stronger than mine. So when the light does not fall upon anything, I cannot say that I exist or that I am displaced to some other place, because there is no place where I go. I have not been switched out. But neither do I cease, neither do I not exist.

When objects appear again, there I will see myself again.

When she lets go of sights, sound, taste, touch, smell, and thought, another attaches to them in her place, which is what I am calling "I" now. Then there are things again. There are things I see and feel and think. Light appears again to be something. I appear again to be something where before I was everywhere and nowhere yet did not appear to be so or appear to be anything at all.

WHEN I WAS VERY YOUNG, most people didn't have electric light because there was no electricity available. That was the first and biggest change in the spirit world. Not only do I say this; it is the opinion of scores of others I know. Without electricity, it's dark at night, simple as that. And when you all live together in the dark, you become open and aware of far more. As your sense doors open wide, your hearing, your touch, taste, smell, your mind and its concocting thoughts and your psychic sense, like a dilating eye in the dark, let so much more in, and consequently you are all the more vulnerable.

People who grew up in the electric light or exposed from infancy to the cathode-ray tube of TV cannot understand this, as this quiet, frightful state is not as deeply seeped into their hearts. People who know the true darkness of night as a child know the fear of ghosts and spirits. The rest of you with electricity cannot even really imagine.

I also certainly and distinctly remember how, when I was a child, my mother would tell me stories of ghosts and spirits in the trees and forests to keep me from wandering off. Well, it worked for a while. And that changes, I think, the way you see the world.

I get a sickening feeling in my stomach that seems to suck my entire body into it, even now, just thinking about Mae Nak Phrakanong. I saw the classic movie (not the new ones) as a little, frightful girl, and I don't know whether I had yet heard the story at the time. Every older person knows the story, though, as Mae Nak is the biggest story of all time in Thailand and has been made into innumerable movies and TV shows. It is a legend handed down, possibly from the past two centuries or longer, but for me, it is mostly little more than an instant, a single image: of one ghostly arm stretching in a bizarre, sickeningly long manner to reach for something that has fallen below a stilted platform house.

That image is burned in my little child mind forever, the child who grew up without electricity and in dark nights and in fear of all the threatening, uncanny entities that my trusted and beloved mother assured me were waiting out there to snatch me. Of course, in truth, it is more than that: all the actual encounters I have had and those of all the others I know. But the image draws everything into it and stands for it all.

Mak believed that he was living with his living wife, Nak, who was, in fact, already dead, but one day, when she wasn't looking, he saw something that chilled him. Mae Nak was preparing food, and something had fallen through the cracks of the platform floor of the house. He saw her reach down to grab it.

Her arm extended to a hideous and unnatural length to reach it.

After that, Mak knew.

He took refuge in the local monastery, but Mae Nak, enraged and distraught, followed him there. The monks encircled Mak with protective string but could not get Nak to go away. Mak was ready to give up his love and attachment to Nang Nak, but she was not similarly prepared.

Then a long series of magical doctors came from near and far to exorcise the spirit, and all were, one by one and in various gruesome ways, defeated and killed by Mae Nak. In the end, it was only the arrival of the powerful Buddhist abbot, Somdet Toh, that could put Mae Nak to rest. He enacted a powerful ritual that put Mae Nak's spirit in a clay vessel, which was then submerged in the river, or else, in another version, he fashioned a magic buckle out of a piece of her skull that he had cracked open, and he carried the piece of skull with him and thus controlled her spirit and was able to send it out and about to do his bidding.

꙳ A love story, sort of. That is perhaps what all such ghost stories are. Ghost stories are sort-of-love-stories. Stories about what can go off about love. About the attachment and hunger of love, love of life, love of others, its tragic and perverse underside.

To be sure, love stories abound of the other type — lovey-dovey stories between young men and young, pure women and complicated by various triangles and circumstances, usually that of the pure woman of lower class hankering after the rich man, who is duped by the mean and petty rich girl, problems that are, in the end, overcome in a luscious embrace (no kissing on TV). There is no shortage of that . . . not at all. But for another side of love, for another perspective, you have to look at ghosts.

And perhaps nothing serves better here than the moment of horror in Mae Nak. It cannot be emphasized enough that this single moment in the story of Mae Nak — on the border between two worlds of love, between, indeed, two realities — is by far the single most iconic moment in Thai movie history. And the most iconic moment of all Thai ghost stories for all time.

Inside the terms of the story, when Mak sees Nak's arm extend, he crosses over from the simulacral reality produced by Nak and their passion to the realization of the real, the real of death and the otherworldly. Previously there were two parallel realities, but they collide, and the horrible truth is revealed. This emphasis in the films of the two parallel realities is a major structure in the form of the Mae Nak story and helps set up the crucial haunting moment.

Film form can work to heighten this masterfully. In the most recent Thai remake of the story, the two parallel realities are heightened through a common Gothic film form technique, the observation of a strictly realist, consistent aesthetics in each version of reality, in this sense from the perspective of Mak on the one hand and everyone else, less possessed, on the other. If done masterfully and linked to the classic, Gothic trick of the real — similar to that which Freud exposed — it can take some time before the audience realizes that the ghost world is not real in the way that the real world is. Usually you realize it before the protagonist does. But in the best-laid tricks of the real, the reveal is simultaneous.

And yet perhaps inhabiting a parallel simultaneity is the continuous realization that both are not real but equally the projections of the cinema. I say "continuous," but, of course, that is very subtly so: for the most part, one might not recognize the unreality of the projected cinematic world but only alight upon it occasionally. And yet that realization must be there also, somewhat continuously, yet often unrecognized, otherwise you might be in absolute terror of the entities on screen. And, then again, if you wanted, perhaps as an experiment or for some other reason, you could decide to consciously recognize it while watching.

Movie film projected on the screen can be thought of in terms of the conventional real: there is a knowing that what one sees is not real, not really there, but where in the real world can you locate that? Where in the real world can you locate the knowing itself, the knowing that something you are watching is not real? Just look. Where is this knowing? What is it? Where is it?

This is, I would insist, the ultimate in *deterrortoreality*.

One can be carried away by the stories, settings, and characters, the sound and sight, but at the same time, "deep down" (in an excavatable space?), we know it is not real. Dig that up. Where is that knowledge? Is it there as you watch? If you do not ask this question, is it there? If you do happen to call it up, from where? And if you call it up, still — where is it? Can you know, sense this?

It might seem that you can't put your finger on it. But, on the other hand, if you call it up, you do you know that you have done so. By this I mean that you must acknowledge that there is a difference between how things are without calling up the thought, "This is not real," and when you do call that thought up.

So you must have some way of knowing its presence. And you do know that you know, right? You can tell the difference, if you follow me, between knowing whether you have called up the question of whether it is real or whether you have not done so. But how do you know if you cannot find that knowledge anywhere? By what means do you know that you know? Where is it, what is it, how is it?

It is precisely this radical turn, toward questioning the source of perceiving itself, that renders the absorptive story of the film world most unreal, and it is the same with anything else. Everything else is unreal in the very same way. Mostly you may see things in the world, or you may seem to see things exclusively. But a sense of perception — a sense that something is happening here, regardless of contents, which we may call perception — is here whether you recognize it or not. What sees either of these?

And similarly the movie screen is there whether you recognize it or not. Mostly you see things, people, actions, story, but in the very process you are also literally seeing the screen. You are always seeing the screen, only most of the time you do not recognize that you are seeing the screen. And you would not be able to see these other things and people without seeing-while-not-recognizing the screen. Everything is made up of screen, consists of screen. There is only screen. No thing can possibly exist that is not of screen.

And you see the screen whether you recognize that or not. What sees either possibility? Can you find *that*?

Refiguring the relationship between, say, ghosts and numbers directs the inquiry toward a possible alternative immateriality to the seeming immateriality of the so-called digitized world, or that of a spirit world, an alternative immateriality suggested first by the evident pointings to it that seemed to issue from number-knowing, future-knowing, and wealth-knowing spirits in Thailand, an alternative Nextworld to the digital future: the one from which all numbers dissolve and from which they come. I realize, of course, that to those most thoroughly caught in the dream, this interest in alternative immaterialities seems fantastic. But since this text, and myself, are not thoroughly real in the habitual, outward, and object-oriented ways through which the real is usually decided, perhaps that might put the mind at ease, just as the spirit stories and rituals themselves might enable, for those who actually participate in them, a willingness to abandon one particular sense of immateriality: the immateriality that tries to eclipse the rest, that "ghost" of numbers and economy that becomes, for some, an obsessional fixation, crowding out all other alternative immaterialities such that one lives completely in a one-dimensional dream, or nightmare rather. The evacuation of the spirit world in favor of an abstracted money world is dangerous and socially disabling as so many have pointed out for so long. And that evacuation seems so real.

Seems so real that I feel unsure about whether the spell can ever be cut. Why are all the neoliberal beings not free?

ɑ I know my place in this text is problematic on so many levels.

But, listen, if I were not here, you would not be here.[1]

I am not going to go away. It will be difficult or impossible for anyone to find a way to stop me, exorcise me, keep me out, now that I have found a way back into your world.

Why do we seem not to be free?

Is there the right desire in the right direction? We spirits have special access to this direction but not so much the desire. For most of us, knowing that the dreamworld is a spell, we can play inside it. It is not a horror for us. The counterspell for the dream is to turn away from it, which we rarely do. Turn away, that is, in precisely the opposite direction, a direction that can only be seen truly by turning the gaze toward the place from which we are looking. And this is precisely the opposite direction that the dreamworld beckons to us from, beckoning us to solve its problems and allay the fears it has itself created. These only require our attention and belief for their power. Withdraw your power from them. Then it is possible to play on them from another angle.

It is true that in my heart I have found precisely this rest, but in another sense, not so. In the sense that I will not, actually, allow myself to rest. I will continue my work and will not stop until you can see what I can see.

Not until you can see it,

That I am the same one as you.

And yet I am not you, and you are not me.

∝ From where I am now, there is nothing else for me to see. If you could know, too, that one's body is just that, just a part of this appearance, this screen . . . this body and that table over there, and that paper, this ink, are all equally a part of this screen world and no more or less so than this body. You cannot know this by looking straight at it, the so-called material world. You have to question the seeing, look to the eye. This world of so-called matter is just one continuity that now takes this shape and then takes another. Always the screen. Form here, form there, the same one. Except here, seemingly in this body, there appears to be an eye, an eye of sorts. Not the physical eye that sees. The one that knows, is awake, taking this in. Where is it? What is it? Is it actually and truly "in" the body, and if not, where could it be? What are its dimensions? Where does it start and stop? Where are its boundaries and limits such that we could call it something? Look, yourself. Where can you find that which is looking? Where are you coming from?

I am not asking you to connect this question to theories of mind or embodiment you have heard, nor ones that you believe, because any thought you have about this is appearing on the screen and is seen, and is not the seer, precisely not what you might be looking for. In other words, you are an audience to the thought of where you are here or where you are coming from, but where is the one who knows that thought? I'm not asking you to decide about whether this is Cartesianism or not or whether that is a good or bad thing. And, of course, this "eye" is not an eye, and it does not "see." But anyway, just look, honestly.

It may seem at first that this eye is somehow tied to or manifest to this so-called material body, and yet it is hard to say where or how. Is it in the head or the torso? It might seem as though it is somewhere between the ears and behind the eyes, but is that not just because one is very attentive to those sense channels? Look closer . . . can you really pinpoint exactly where it is coming from? And yet it seems to be there, here, somewhere — the knowing. And it seems as though it is from here that one can see both what appears to be a "material" world of which one's body is an indissoluble part and this searching itself — that, too, is perceived. Perceived from a disembodied eye, strangely also tied somehow to this body, yet not really of it, not in the sense that there is any particular reason or way that one can find for why or how this eye is here, or where in "here" it is.

This is because it has no place, and it is not a thing. It is not yours, or your mind's, or as though there was any actually existing thing we could call a mind. Not even here and now is this text in your personal mind. It may seem as though this is your mind, that it is in your personal mind that this is happening. That I am speaking to you in your personal mind. I am a voice in your mind. Or it may seem as though you have entered the mind of another, my mind, or that of my host, the writer (the "real" person here). No one of these is true.

The sameness between you and I . . . it is not here, there, it is not anywhere. It has no form. No sound, no smell, no taste, no sight, no touch, no thought: it can only know such things, but as soon as you turn to it itself, you cannot find it, because in order to know it, there would have to be a knowing there, to know the knowing, and so then what would be the shape or form of that? If you knew . . . then there would have to be another knowing there.

You see, we already are, from the start, without territory or terrain and always were.

It may seem difficult to see this, but it is the most important and simplest thing: that you and I are the same one . . . bottomless, radiant, nowhere, without limits.

ONE OF MY LAST POSSESSIONS, or so they told me, was completely unexpected and amazing. I went through the usual ceremony. I held up the *khan* and offered myself up to the *dek guman*, but I began to shake violently, dry heave, and almost throw up, as though I were a novice medium again. And then, suddenly, I had a booming voice move through me, or so they told me, a voice that exploded in laughter. They said the jow identified himself as Jow Paw Taan Hin. The Spirit of the Lignite Coal.

He said, "Give me green and red robes. Bring me my headscarf." His voice was deep and loud, and coming from my little body, it must have been quite startling. Everyone ran this way and that trying to find outfits that Jow Paw Taan Hin would be satisfied with. Eventually he was, and he warmed up to them, listening to everyone's problems. They told him of how all the money had dried up, and he nodded. They told him of the deaths and murders, of the hauntings and possessions, of the debts and the loss of the land. They told him of the threats and that the syndicate was moving in, closing in, that things were getting tighter, that they were holding on to their plots of land but were on the verge of losing everything and maybe also their lives. Nodding. Hmm. Hmm. Deep, rumbling concern. Then he suddenly burst again into hearty laughter.

"Don't worry, don't worry. Good fortune is coming. Great fortune is coming. Huge mountains of fortune are coming! I will take care of it all. I will take care of you all."

This was what I was told of the greatest possession séance I ever had. It was legendary, and it is still talked about to this day. There are not so many people that remember all the details of my story anymore. But many people remember that one day in my life. The amazing day when the Spirit of the Lignite Coal came and took my body and announced himself to us all and filled everyone with the rumblings of his deep, disturbing laughter that was nevertheless contagious and relieving as well.

⚘ It was at this point, when my fortunes were at their height, that the little dek guman issued his most certain and urgent number. It was 149. He told everyone to play it straight for whatever they could afford. Because I was so famous as a medium at the time, it wasn't just people who came to see the Little Prince who played 149. It spread everywhere in our village. The rumor that the dek guman said to put it all on 149 straight — or sometimes they said 148 or 199 or some other number, but mostly 149 — spread intact not only in our village but also into Lampang Town, to Chiang Mai, throughout the whole region, to Bangkok, and even to distant parts of the kingdom.

But, of course, the greatest concentration of 149 was in our area and among my people. Ba Jae saw to that. She and my mother became incredibly obsessed with 149. Everywhere they went, they said to play it. Ba Jae made frequent trips to Lampang Town to spread stories about 149, inventing every sort of correspondence and meaning related to one, to four, and to nine and all kinds of stories about how our village was becoming rich because of our dek guman. And every time the dek guman came to my body, he backed her up, telling everyone to play 149 straight. People lined up at our shrine to bring gifts of candy, toys, snacks, and all kinds of money. Long lines and crowded seances filled with bubbling laughter and joy and the greatest expectations of fortune. Even rich people from town came in pickup trucks, and even one Mercedes Benz came, all covered in dusty dried mud, bringing a television set. The first one in our village. Soon people crowded our house to watch television at night, which only brought more people together to talk about 149. And then they would return to crowd our house during the day to see the Little Prince.

In the past sometimes there would be periods where the gifts would come in a great hoard, but that was always after a successful round of lottery. Never before did such gifts come before the drawing and at a time when people had such little to give.

But they did believe in . . . "me," or the spirit in me, that there was a special communicative connection in the fact that I was not completely of this world, this world of so much trouble, of fear, that I was issuing from beyond it. That "I," as the spirit, was perceiving it all on another level, from another place, free from fear, innocent as a child, and in proper account with the dead, beyond all haunting, because a spirit cannot possess itself any more than a ghost can haunt itself. How could I, as the boy-prince spirit, fear the realm of immateriality and the source of numbers when I was, in effect, the very same thing as that realm itself? For this reason, I have special access to the numbers. The source of all value is the same as the source of all thought. It is us. And we are not a thing. Only those with a recognition close to the source of it all know this.

We cannot be counted, not in truth. In truth, we are beyond the subjection of numbers. We are. And we are without need of counting.

And yet, as the spirit, well he could still count if he wanted, to play, to draw in childlike spirit ways from this realm, because he was innocent of it as well.

Numbers, money: there is nothing in them themselves that is wrong, intrinsically. It is simply believing in the dreamworld they evoke where all the trouble lies. Once you are one, then there are two and more, and then there are others, and because this one must be protected, these others cannot be trusted.

But here, now, in a spirit that has merged its sense of itself, at least in part, back into the source, there was trust.

And, of course, never before had the trade in unofficial lottery reached the levels it then did, at least in those days. Our village was the hotbed of the action, and this news eventually reached the highest levels of the mafia racket. That it was our village that was spurring everyone on.

To the rackets in Bangkok and other places, there would, of course, not be any knowledge about our region, our village, and certainly not me.

At any given drawing, there were hundreds of hot numbers, whose fame arose by who knows what means and from who knows what source. Number rumors tilted and swayed in storms or died out in calms like ships cast adrift in a turbulent sea. The rise and fall of stories, explanations, uncanny correspondences, represented a field seemingly more random than that of drawing random numbers themselves. And there was no way for the racket to know what numbers were actually being played or how much was actually being bet. It was all on paper. It was all speculative. It was all handled by individual dealers that kept their own books.

Our local Lampang jow paw also had no way of knowing exactly how much was being bet, and on what numbers either. But eventually enough people began talking about the huge bets and the huge profits that the lottery dealers were set to make that the godfathers did find out not only about tremendous spike in bets placed but also about 149 and, eventually, even about me. That there was a girl, a girl that everyone believed in. That the whole rural countryside had gone crazy about this girl, prophet, medium, or something, whom they all believed knew the numbers. They had to have been happy about the huge fortune that was about to fall in their laps, all because the villagers had finally freaked out and gone off the deep end. Probably they were even proud of themselves for what they had done to us, pushed us to the point of desperation, where almost everyone everywhere had put their hopes in 149.

But, then again, they were ordinary flesh and blood, people just like us. They must have clutched their Buddhist amulets and lucky charms with white knuckles. They did their good-luck rituals. Not that they would have believed in me. But one never knows. Everything, absolutely everything about gambling, whether placing or taking bets, is . . . well, such a gamble. No one feels as though they have their feet on the ground.

Ba Jae, too, was gambling. I don't know whether she even put down one baht on 149. But she was gambling on the fact that the godfathers would not believe. That they would see us as silly little superstitious peasants. That they would do nothing to stop us, would not seek me out, or Ba Jae, that they would see this as the final end to these women stirring up trouble in some village somewhere in outer Lampang.

Lottery Day

On lottery day, I sat next to my Mother and Ba Jae. My mother, as usual, was full of expectation, hope, and glee. She was never so happy as on lottery day as the drawing time was winding near, and she would arrange her slips of paper first this way then that. This time she was happier than ever and having more fun because, for the first time, we did not listen on the radio but watched on this brand-new TV that was set to the drawing. I got dizzy watching the balls floating and spinning in the wheel. Everyone else, practically the whole village, in our house and spilling out into the lane, was filled with excitement about the biggest drawing ever. But Ba Jae was perfectly calm. No anticipation. No excitement. She looked more like one of the cold, calculated assassins in the American movies. She had no moustache, of course, but the look in her eye was like a killer focusing on his defenseless prey.

The first of the last three balls — the ones that count — dropped, and everyone but Ba Jae cheered: it was a 1. The next ball would be the key. Of course, one number right did not mean much. That happens all the time. Then the next ball dropped: 4. Everyone's hearts must have stopped. This was it. Either the last ball dropped and made the three-digit sequence, or it did not, and the first two numbers would mean nothing. It was now all or nothing as people lurched in silence, so many people silent and focused as one mind and heart.

The last ball fell, and it was a 9, indeed.

If there were hoards of gifts before the drawing, I don't know what to call what happened afterward. Our village went crazy with joy. Dancing, music, drinking. A couple of people died in accidents. Even the lottery dealers, who had lost their commission that week, joined in. It was a beautiful day and an amazing night, all night long, for our village.

But they had little consciousness of just how big an event this was for the entire region and how uncertain everything was now that the numbers had come out 1-4-9.

People brought gifts, money and gold, to my house and waited in long lines for the dek guman to come so that they could express their gratitude.

But these gifts never did reach their destination.

I tried and tried, but the dek guman did not come back. Everything in those few days was off-kilter. People went to collect their winnings. At first there were payouts, but then the payouts dried up. The godfathers, it was rumored, could not back all the bets that had come in. They were pulling out. The dealers became the objects of rage and had to hide out for several days before everyone cooled down and realized the enormity of what had just happened and why there were no payouts.

The bank of the godfathers had been almost broken, but they were, in fact, beaten back. In a way, that was, of course, not all bad news.

But nothing was working right anymore. Some people could not get their winnings while others who got large sums of money could not repay the Little Prince because he would not come back to me.

I tried and tried, but he would not come down. People got frustrated and angry with me. They said I must have committed sins and talked about all kinds of terrible things that I must have done to make my body impure, an unclean place for the Little Prince to reside, things a little girl like me never even thought about.

ଔ I was in trouble. Big trouble. And one day I could feel it, hear it. Motorcycles were gunning their throttles from distant points in the village. I spied one, a pair of strange men riding together, tearing holes in the red-dirt of a village path. Dark was setting in, but they still had their sunglasses on. Somehow I knew not to let them see me.

But others saw me, and it was as if I were a worse thing than the godfathers' men tearing loose on our village. Everyone was closing their shutters as I walked by. Everyone looked at me with terror. Did they think I was the Tree Woman? It was me, but they were having none of it. As I walked down one teak-fenced alley, I got a shock when suddenly a very old man poked his head around a corner, his eyes wide and crazy, his look bearing down on me. "Get out of here, little girl! It's you they want."

Before I knew what happened, he was gone again.

My heart was pounding and my guts sinking by the time I got to Ba Jae's house, and I ran in and saw my mother there, who looked at me with fear.

"What is that? What is happening? Why is everyone hiding?" I blurted out.

"They know," Ba Jae said. "They know about what we have been up to. They know all about you, about what has been happening here. And I think they believe in you now."

I could see the fear in her eyes, and I felt sorry for her. And for my mother too. The men would be coming after us. After scaring up the neighborhood, they would certainly come find us here. And now that they believed in my power, they would certainly come to squash it out.

Ba Jae and my mother spoke heatedly about various plans. We could go far away to Chiang Mai. We could go to Bangkok. But they had little cash or gold. As they spoke and spoke, I became increasingly doubtful. My poor mother could not exist in a big town, I knew that. And they could find us in Chiang Mai.

It became clear, in the mind of the girl I was at that time, that I was the cause of it all. If they didn't have me to protect, there would be no danger. It was me they were after. It was me who had to go.

But as a small girl, I could not think of any good plan of where to go or where to turn. I had already done everything I could, everything that was asked of me. There was nowhere for me to go but out to the trees. I would make my way out there all alone. As Ba Jae and my mother hatched out various plans, I slipped out undetected.

I slipped out of the village and, I thought, also into the forest undetected, but apparently I was wrong about that. Soon I could hear them, the men, coming for me. But I didn't run except to get to where I was going, before they got there. In fact I had the overwhelming feeling that it was best this way. That this is how it should end, and all would be well. So I let them follow me.

I had no fear of the forest anymore. I wanted to be there. It was where I wanted to go. To the trees. Whatever might become of me, I wanted to be in the trees, and, in fact, somewhere in my mind, I knew exactly what was going to happen to me and that I was heading toward one tree in particular, to her.

The world of the village and all their problems, which had sucked me in and chewed me up and now seemed to be on the verge of swallowing me whole . . . I had enough of all that, and so I walked through forest, patches of clear sky hanging from a full moon, my dear friend moon, who lit the way for me, and I felt the soft red dirt of the path underfoot and then finally slipped almost silently into a boat and paddled on the still water, all sounds from the surface of the water dissolving into one and rising from that stillness the bare and ordinary presence of the world.

And so, that is where I ended up. At the tree, with her. That is where my life among you ended. That is where their men tracked me down and caught me, got me. That is where I died, where my blood soaked into the earth and into the roots of her tree. The biggest, strangest tree in the forest. Surrounded by all the other trees, among them all but not of them.

In the end I was caught by the stories. I suppose I had been seen heading out to the forest, and they were able to guess where I might go, what with the tales everyone was telling all the time about me and her.

I did it out of love and out of a calling that I truthfully cannot explain. It is not that I wanted to die. But I wanted the others to live, and somehow a certainty arose in me that, in any case, I would die before I died. That my own imprisonment in myself would end at last, that this was what it had all been about from the beginning. And so to return to the tree, no matter who followed, this was a return that was irrevocable.

I just knew, somehow, of the possibility to be free, and I went for it. Something the others around me could not do, for they were still mucking about in games, games that I knew, without doubt, I had finally left behind.

But I would happily take the blame for it all, take the fall, and let all that trouble disappear into the traces and memories left behind of the girl-prophet, or whatever it is they might remember me by. Because I knew I had no more need of all that, any of that.

ONE OF EARLIEST INTERNATIONAL PROTESTS in the formative period of anti-World Bank activism in the world was that against the Mae Moh power plant, which was to generate electrical power from lignite strip mines, destroying the landscape, uprooting tens of thousands of peasants, and filling the air with sulfur and other pollutants from its rich black smoke that would descend heavily on flora, fauna, and people for miles around. The protests against Mae Moh, which failed, are now long forgotten on the world stage of things. Huge loans were dispersed from the World Bank, and the plant was built.

Just as everything in our sick, assaulted village was about to crumble, the Thai State, in cooperation with the international lending and development community, pumped giant sums of money into the area. And just as the jow paw were set to get their hands on everything we had, our village was forcibly seized by the state instead. But everyone was given a large sum of cash to build a new house and a perfectly square plot of land in what was to be our new, relocated village some miles out from the site of the new power plant. All the formal titles to land were defunct, and the informal titles now meaningless.

Many of the men were put to work in construction, and many with education, like samanera and monks who disrobed and those who had the fortune to attend and finish middle school in Lampang Town, were trained as technicians for the plant. These men became, by our standards at the time, fairly wealthy.

But although the men were the first to get in on the salaried work and decent union jobs at the plant, it was not long before the women were able to draw them into their circles of loans. Not to mention, after all, the fact that there were a lot of loans still outstanding. Much of the new extra money went to Ba Jae, who got many of her loans back with a significant portion of the interest due. She made deals and forgiveness pacts with many of her debtors. In no time she was flush again, and so were the women in her circle.

And the desire for loans was not diminished by the new prosperity. Quite the contrary. There were hundreds of people hungry for loans, wanting to build really nice houses, the houses of their dreams, on their new plots of land arranged in square grid rows on perfectly straight roads to be paved by the power authorities.

And all this demand came right after the syndicate had been hit up for most of their cash. They did not get the land. They did not take over the gambling nor the lending.

They had no money to pay their network of police and debt enforcers, who had to be disbanded for a time. No money to back lottery bets. No loan money. And they could not buy the land now, even if they had the cash, which they did not.

It was many years before they could come back into force. But by that time, the new village was prosperous and the godfathers had no use for this land. There were money, gambling, and lending everywhere, and although the daily loans came back, there was just no way of preventing the cash from flowing into and through the godmother circles — there was just so much of it about. The men on motorcycles did come back to work the daily loans, but the worst of the aggression was gone. The godmothers kept guns at home, but no one ever had to use them on an attacker. At worst, there were a few incidents of firing in the air. There was an understanding that the godmothers and godfathers would each have their niche and their place. Ba Jae did not follow up on any more plans to expand her interests, to own large plots of land or develop any kind of super marketplace. But neither did the godfathers' big ceramic factory materialize. In fact, in the land and villages that the state did not seize, ceramics became a cottage industry that grew from small family businesses into large work-shops dotting the villagescape and bringing in more outside money in a distributed pattern. Meanwhile Ba Jae kept strictly to the money trade, but she became richer, far richer than anyone would have suspected possible even way back when things were, now so long ago, going well.

And the spirits — what parties they had! Huge spirit parties with music played by large bands hooked up to electrical power. Dancing, drinking, and smoking the day away. There were more spirits than ever before. All kinds of spirits from all times in history and all places. Jow Paw Hin Taan came and took several medium bodies in the area on a regular basis, laughing and laughing, here, there, everywhere.

Sure, there was the smokestack air that Jow Paw Hin Taan brought and that they all had to breathe. There were the rashes, and the crops burned out by noxious gasses descending to the earth, and the huge gashing wounds cut into the hills. And, of course, there were all the cancer deaths, taking so many innocent people while still in their forties and fifties. Not just the workers but their families and other people in the area. All that death. But there was money too. All the death and all the funerals and all the casinos and all the money. Money and new life and new deaths for everyone.

Even for me. I had a new kind of life as well.

⚶ Listen. You might think I am unreal, but here I am, in your life right now.

I am a part of you now, and you are a part of me.

The past and the future are not here now, are not real. You may or may not go back to those you know, to that which you think is the real. Probably you will. Probably you will not die right now or in the next moment. But you might. The only thing you know for sure is that right now you are here with me. You are a part of me, and I am a part of you. The only real things are you and me.

Listen. If I did not exist, you would not exist.

⚶ If I could tell you what I am, I would. Or where in this world or the next I am to be placed . . . dreamed, written, or possessed. But if you offer me a body, I will enter it. The rest is make-believe.

If you knew just what I am, then you would know the answer to all our problems. You would know to what we all owe our promises, what will give us cure and excise the unruly dreams and crooked staples of reason lodged into our brains.

   A drizzling night it became, but still moonlit. Always eyeing the moon, that is me. I am kneeling at the foot of the teak tree. The giant one, and I know how horribly its corpse would look were it to be cut down and placed at the foot of a house that some general or mafia boss has built on farmer's land. With nowhere to turn, I have slipped unnoticed from my mother's gaze and have snuck out from the village, made my way through the forest to this, my resting place, my tree.

There is nothing that can be done except lodge into the very fiber of its being even a trace of the magic that may someday save it and our souls as well. They will be coming for you, tree. They want to kill you and get into this earth, this clay, and eat it all up.

We are not going to give up easily. This tree and I. You have protected me all these years, and now I must do my duty as a daughter to her mother. My horrible, lovely other mother.

My hair is soaked, my clothes are soaked, and the drizzle almost beats on my skin as water flows over my body. There is nothing left of our human world to separate me from water, from the elements, and from the blue-blackness of the darker night lit now only by the slightest trickle of moon and some distant field where men fish the flooded puddles that line the red-dirt road, drunk and loud, by lamplight. Or is that what the sound is? Is it anything but simply sound?

And then, as the glow of flashlights grasps the details of branch, leaf, and bramble around me, I do not heed the insistence of the light, to turn my head to their source, nor to the bootsteps' splitter-splatter, pattering through slimy leaves, drawing closer to my body. I hear it all as though it were music.

Then single sounds without meaning. Single sparkles of light and dark, light and dark. My hand raises to brush hair from my eyes as if by its own volition, and the hand moves

one

single

moment

at

a

time.

Fragments of motion that each take forever. Forever full and then instantly gone again. But my hand never makes it to the hair over my eyes.

It is too late for me to need to see anything with my eyes. It is too late for me to startle at the crack of a violent sound. Just one moment of sound after another, and sensing that my end is near is no different than this touch ends, and there is another; this pain ends, and then there is another; this darkness ends, and then there is light; this clear light ends, and there it is again. I am, all along and forever and ever.

NOTES

1 · The Ghost Manifesto

1 One might think that the anthropology of fantasy might be of use here, but this work does not seriously challenge the reality status of anthropology itself. While fantasy is a category that appears in anthropological scholarship, it has never to my knowledge been the case that any anthropological approach to fantasy has questioned its own reality status. It is always "real fantasies" that are the objects of study.

2 Žižek, *Looking Awry*, 22–23.

3 Hardt and Negri, *Empire*.

4 Cameron, "Indigenous Spectrality." Note that while some will read into her position only a prohibition on spectrality, using standard politico-aesthetic templates, her text is clearly about opening possibilities that are politically different than what has come before.

5 Smith, *The Wealth of Nations*.

6 Boellstorff, "For Whom the Ontology Turns," 387–407.

7 Klima, "Thai Love Thai," 448.

8 Barad, "Posthumanist Performativity," 801.

9 Barad, "Posthumanist Performativity," 802.

10 Barad, "Posthumanist Performativity," 810.

11 I am using "representationalism" at the moment in the same or similar usage as in Barad's text. More commonly, it is taken in philosophy to mean the position of af-

firming a world out there that is real but that is only known as mental or subjective thought or image and so might require a rigorous process of getting knowledge to correspond with or resemble that reality out there or, in the extreme "constructionist" or "cultural" version, renders that task impossible.

12 Derrida, *Specters of Marx*.

13 Derrida, *Specters of Marx*, xviii–xix.

14 Davis, "Hauntology, Spectres and Phantoms," 373.

15 Derrida, *Of Grammatology*.

16 Jameson, "Marx's Purloined Letter," 373.

17 Loevlie, "Faith in the Ghosts of Literature."

18 Loevlie, "Faith in the Ghosts of Literature," 337.

19 Loevlie, "Faith in the Ghosts of Literature," 337.

20 Loevlie, "Faith in the Ghosts of Literature," 334.

21 Gordon, *Ghostly Matters*, 7.

22 Gordon, *Ghostly Matters*, 25.

23 Gordon, *Ghostly Matters*, 20.

24 Gordon, *Ghostly Matters*, 20

25 Gordon, *Ghostly Matters*, 10.

26 Gordon, *Ghostly Matters*, 23–24.

27 Gordon, *Ghostly Matters*, 19.

28 Gordon, *Ghostly Matters*, 26.

29 Derrida, "A 'Madness' Must Watch Over Thinking," 347.

30 Loevlie, "Faith in the Ghosts of Literature," 38.

31 Derrida, "Signature, Event, Context," 91.

32 Loevlie, "Faith in the Ghosts of Literature," 347–48.

33 Perhaps this is more like what Stuart McLean fabulates about anthropology in *Fictionalizing Anthropology* when he says that "anthropology's most radical potential consists — and has always consisted — of its capacity to undermine conventional distinctions between documentary and fiction. By collapsing the representational distance on which such distinctions depend, reality — and not just human beings' culturally circumscribed representations of it — is rendered open to questioning and, potentially, refashioning" (*Fictionalizing Anthropology*, xi). Perhaps, or perhaps not, what radical anthropology has "always consisted" of, but certainly a radical imagination about that!

34 Freud was speaking specifically of scary stories that are presented as being true but instead are revealed to be made up, thus giving cheap, uncanny effects. See the next chapter for more on Freud's separations of fiction and reality and how important they are for his analysis. Freud, "The 'Uncanny,'" 217–56.

35 Derrida, *Specters of Marx*, 291.

36 Wachowski and Wachowski, *The Matrix*.

2 · World Gothic

1   Nonzee, *Nang Nak*.
2   Chakrabarty, *Provincializing Europe*.
3   Freud, "The 'Uncanny,'" 156.
4   Freud, "The 'Uncanny,'" 156; emphasis in original.
5   Freud, "The 'Uncanny,'" 156.
6   Freud, "The 'Uncanny,'" 157.
7   Freud, "The 'Uncanny,'" 157; emphasis in original.
8   Freud, "The 'Uncanny,'" 158.
9   Freud, "The 'Uncanny,'" 158.
10 Freud, "The 'Uncanny,'" 159.
11 Freud, "The 'Uncanny,'" 159.
12 Freud, "The 'Uncanny,'" 159.
13 Freud, "The 'Uncanny,'" 159.
14 Whorf, *Language, Thought and Reality*, 134–59.
15 Nakata, *Ringu*.
16 The original website and URL for this report are no longer available or searchable.
17 Duffield, *Ghost of Mae Nak*. See box-office totals at https://www.boxofficemojo.com/movies/intl/?page=&country=TH&id=_fGHOSTOFMAENAK01.

3 · Betting on the Real

1   Deleuze and Guattari, *A Thousand Plateaus*; Hardt and Negri, *Empire*.
2   Hardt and Negri, *Empire*, 346–37.
3   Hardt and Negri, *Empire*, 347.
4   Hardt and Negri, *Empire*, 346.
5   Hardt and Negri, *Empire*, 345–47.
6   Hardt and Negri, *Empire*, 347.
7   Hardt and Negri, *Empire*, 347
8   Deleuze and Guattari, *A Thousand Plateaus*.
9   See Massumi, *Parables for the Virtual*.
10 Clarke, "Hazards of Prophecy."
11 The epitome of this would be Jean and John Comaroff's conceptions of "Occult Economies" and "Millenial Capitalism" in their articles of the same titles, however laudable this work is in its attempt to take up the mantle of speculative imagination in the exploration of emergent futures.
12 Belo and Rosenfeld, *Dragons in Distress*; Godemont, *The New Asian Renaissance*; Henderson, *Asia Falling*; Kulick and Wilson, *Thailand's Turn*; Robison and Goodman, *The New Rich in Asia*; Rower, *Asia Rising*; Yu, *Asia's New World Order*. The eco-

nomic commentary flips in 1997, exchanging positive for negative valences of a stable "latent structure of orientalism" as explained by Said, *Orientalism*. Of course, the discourse is carried far more pervasively in innumerable press reports, editorials, and academic articles, not to mention, to a lesser degree, in novels and films. There is no space to begin to capture this discourse here.

13 Again, in international economic discourse more broadly, there are always naysayers for good reason. But it would be a vast distortion to claim that the financial panic of the latter half of 1997 was specifically anticipated in terms of its scale. By definition, a panic is unexpected. There could be no massive disinvestment without a prior investment.

14 For the classic, see Wittfogel, *Oriental Despotism*.

15 Weber, *The Protestant Ethic and the Spirit of Capitalism*, 49; cf. Taussig, "The Sun Gives without Receiving," 394.

16 See Klima, *The Funeral Casino*.

17 As long as a significant number of forecasts and analyses are hedged bets, open to retrospective interpretation in a variety of manners, then the realm from which those insights into reality are issued will also continue to remain authoritative. Individuals and groups within this realm can rise and fall in moral capital and can win or lose, but the realm itself, and the terms with which the forecasters operate, always wins, and the monopoly stranglehold on the authority to speak on matters of money remains in place. In the gambles of forecasting, there were many big losers but also some big winners. In economics, for instance, take Paul Krugman, whose famous hero-with-clay-feet argument, "The Myth of Asia's Miracle," while not predicting the exact mechanism of decline of Asian economies nor, as the author later admitted, coming even close to predicting the sheer scale of the decline, nevertheless came out at just the right time to seem prophetic, which even the author himself, though not averse to all the moral capital it afforded, admitted was somewhat coincidental. But as long as there are a variety of forecasts, or in other words, as long as there are a variety of economists, some are going to be right, and thus the authority to speak on these matters will not be lost from this realm. It is not necessary to take a position on the question of whether classical or neoclassical economics is really a scientific discipline or whether the discipline actually apprehends the natural realities of economic phenomena (indeed, recent critical anthropology's engagement with economics has been flippant, to say the least). Regardless of, or in addition to, any degree of accurate and practical knowledge produced, the authority to speak and pronounce on these matters both produces and depends upon, in part, forms of prophetic authority.

18 IMF, "The IMF's Response to the Asian Crisis."

19 Few of the IMF's policies wound up having had a positive effect, and the steadily building anti-IMF sentiment long brewing in both ultraconservative and radical circles erupted in the center when the organization thoroughly discredited itself

with its seriously flawed "solutions." The short explanation is that the IMF applied its "structural adjustment" policies on the Asian states rather than focus on the private corporations who were the ones in debt. The states, in most cases, did not carry heavy public-sector debt, and thus the IMF pinched off the only viable source of liquidity and spending, adding severe economic depression to an already difficult situation. The fact that they had the free hand to do this, despite the fact that many highly respected economists (in many cases using thought processes that are generally considered common sense in economics) were screaming on the sidelines while the IMF did as it pleased, says a lot about how powerfully moral authority can accumulate. In this case, the prophetic authority undid itself by not hedging its bet.

5 · Regendered Debt

1   In light of this "global capitalism," it is important to first understand, as Saskia Sassen in "Spatialities and Temporalities of the Global" argues in her meticulously cautious fashion, that the "global" as such *does not really exist*, insofar as it does not yet encompass anything near truly worldwide in range, nor does it, in the dimension of depth, necessarily permeate the subjective lifeworlds of social reality as it is lived for a significant number of people, a dimension that is particularly difficult for her scale of analysis to assess. Sassen contends that — despite the ostensive zero-sum game between state and global forces — state institutions are important mechanisms for the spread of global processes.

2   In Thai, *jow* has a wide range of uses, and can mean "lord," as in feudal arrangements, or "boss" in a corporation, or it can be an honorific prefix or suffix to the name of gods, of a monotheistic God, or of the Buddha, among other uses. *Mae* means "mother." Leaders of crime syndicates are called *jow paw*, associating *jow* with the word for "father" (*paw*). The English "godfather," as used in the crime novels of Mario Puzo, is translated into Thai as *jow paw*. For these reasons, "godmother" in the context of this article is a meaningful translation for *jow mae*.

7 · The Godfathers

1   The dominance of "the economy" in national discourse has also had some positive effects, such as a greater chance for issues of economic justice to attain the status of public relevancy. These issues are perhaps less excluded now than ever before.

2   See Klima, *The Funeral Casino*.

3   The assemblage of money for public display on a tree is a long-standing tradition in Buddhist donation ceremony in Thailand, associating money with the growth of

life and with the enlightenment of the Buddha under the shade and protection of a Bo tree. "Merit," or *puñña* in Pali and *bun* in Thai, is the spiritual benefit accrued by the connection established between giver and deserved receiver in alms giving, connecting the benefit of the monk's or recipient's moral life to those who support it and spreading the benefit accrued to relatives, to the dead, or to others who are connected to the giver. This intersubjective kamma, sprouting in all directions through the money tree, has become a central ritual practice in postcrash Thailand in massive donation ceremonies led by the famed forest monk Luangta Maha Bua, in which millions of dollars in money trees are given through Luangta to the Thai national currency reserve (for more, see Klima, "Thai Love Thai").

4 Bataille, *The Accursed Share*, vol. 1.

12 · Everywhere and Nowhere

1 The form of expression in this passage of text is inspired by Longchepa, *You Are the Eyes of the World*.

BIBLIOGRAPHY

Barad, Karen. "Posthumanist Performativity: Toward an Understanding of How Matter Comes to Matter." *Signs* 28, no. 3 (2003): 801–31.

Bataille, Georges. *The Accursed Share.* Vol. 1. Translated by Robert Hurley. New York: Zone, 1991.

Belo, Walden, and Stephanie Rosenfeld. *Dragons in Distress: Asia's Miracle Economies in Crisis.* Oakland, CA: Food First, 1998.

Boellstorff, Tom. "For Whom the Ontology Turns: Theorizing the Digital Real." *Current Anthropology* 57, no. 4 (2016): 387–407.

Cameron, Emilie. "Indigenous Spectrality and the Politics of Postcolonial Ghost Stories." *Cultural Geographies*, no. 15 (2008): 383–93.

Chakrabarty, Dipesh. *Provincializing Europe: Postcolonial Thought and Historical Difference.* 2nd ed. Princeton, NJ: Princeton University Press, 1997.

Clarke, Arthur C. "Hazards of Prophecy: The Failure of Imagination." In *Profiles of the Future,* rev. ed. New York: Orion, 1973.

Comaroff, Jean, and John L. Comaroff. "Millennial Capitalism: First Thoughts on a Second Coming." *Public Culture* 12, no. 2 (2000): 291–343.

Comaroff, Jean, and John L. Comaroff. "Occult Economies and the Violence of Abstraction: Notes from the South African Postcolony." *American Ethnologist* 26, no. 2 (1999): 279–303.

Comaroff, Joshua. "Ghostly Topographies: Landscape and Biopower in Modern Singapore." *Cultural Geographies* 14 (2007): 56–73.

Davis, Colin. "Hauntology, Spectres and Phantoms." *French Studies* 59, no. 3 (2005): 373–79.

Deleuze, Gilles, and Félix Guattari. *A Thousand Plateaus: Capitalism and Schizophrenia*. Translated by Brian Massumi. Minneapolis: University of Minnesota Press, 1987.

Derrida, Jacques. "A 'Madness' Must Watch Over Thinking." In *Points . . . Interviews 1974–1994*, translated by Peggy Kamuf, 339–65. Stanford, CA: Stanford University Press, 1995.

Derrida, Jacques. *Of Grammatology*. Baltimore: Johns Hopkins University Press, 1998.

Derrida, Jacques. "Signature, Event, Context." In *A Derrida Reader*, 80–111. New York: Columbia University Press, 1991.

Derrida, Jacques. *Specters of Marx: The State of the Debt, the Work of Mourning, and the New International*. Translated by Peggy Kamuf. New York: Routledge, 1994.

Duffield, Mark. *Ghost of Mae Nak*. Box Office Entertainment, 2005.

Freud, Sigmund. "The 'Uncanny.'" In *On Creativity and the Unconscious*, 122–61. New York: Harper, 1958.

Godement, François. *The New Asian Renaissance: From Colonialism to the Post-Cold War*. Translated by Elisabeth J. Parcell. New York: Routledge, 1996.

Gordon, Avery. *Ghostly Matters*. 2nd ed. Minneapolis: University of Minnesota Press, 2008.

Hardt, Michael, and Antonio Negri. *Empire*. Cambridge, MA: Harvard University Press, 2000.

Henderson, Callum. *Asia Falling: Making Sense of the Asian Currency Crisis and Its Aftermath*. New York: McGraw-Hill, 1998.

IMF (International Monetary Fund). "The IMF's Response to the Asian Crisis: A Factsheet." Consulted January 2005. http://www.imf.org/external/np/exr/facts/asia.htm.

Jameson, Fredric. "Marx's Purloined Letter." *New Left Review* 1, no. 209 (1995): 75–109.

Klima, Alan. *The Funeral Casino: Meditation, Massacre, and Exchange with the Dead in Thailand*. Princeton, NJ: Princeton University Press, 2002.

Klima, Alan. *Ghosts and Numbers*. Cambridge, MA: Documentary Educational Resources, 2010.

Klima, Alan. "Spirits of Dark Finance: A Local Hazard for the International Moral Fund." *Cultural Dynamics*, no. 1 (2006): 33–60.

Klima, Alan. "Thai Love Thai: Financing Emotion in Post-Crash Thailand." *Ethnos* 69, no. 4 (2006): 451–71.

Krugman, Paul. "The Myth of Asia's Miracle." *Foreign Affairs* (November–December 1994): 62–78.

Kulick, Elliot F., and Don Wilson. *Thailand's Turn: Profile of a New Dragon*. New York: St. Martin's, 1994.

Loevlie, Elisabeth M. "Faith in the Ghosts of Literature: Poetic Hauntology in Derrida, Blanchot and Morrison's *Beloved*." *Religions*, no. 4 (2013): 336–50.

Longchenpa. *You Are the Eyes of the World*. Translated by Kennard Lipman and Merrill Peterson. Ithaca, NY: Snow Lion, 2000.

Massumi, Brian. *Parables for the Virtual: Movement, Affect, Sensation*. Durham, NC: Duke University Press, 2002.

Mauss, Marcel. *The Gift*. Translated by W. D. Halls. New York: W. W. Norton, 1990.

McLean, Stuart. *Fictionalizing Anthropology: Encounters and Fabulations at the Edges of the Human*. Minneapolis: University of Minnesota Press, 2017.

Nakata, Hideo. *Ringu (The Ring)*. Dreamworks Video, 1999.

Nonzee, Nimibutr. *Nang Nak*. Buddy Film and Video, 1997.

Robison, Richard, and David S. Goodman, eds. *The New Rich in Asia: Mobile Phones, McDonalds and Middle-Class Revolution*. New York: Routledge, 1996.

Rower, Jim. *Asia Rising: Why America Will Prosper as Asia's Economies Boom*. New York: Simon & Schuster, 1996.

Said, Edward. *Orientalism*. New York: Knopf, 1979.

Sassen, Saskia. "Spatialities and Temporalities of the Global: Elements for a Theorization." *Public Culture* 12, no. 1 (2002): 215–32.

Smith, Adam. *The Wealth of Nations*. New York: Modern Library, 2000.

Stoler, A. L., ed. *Haunted by Empire: Geographies of Intimacy in North American History*. Durham, NC: Duke University Press, 2006.

Strange, Susan. *Casino Capitalism*. Manchester: Manchester University Press, 1986.

Taussig, Michael. "The Sun Gives without Receiving: An Old Story." *Comparative Studies of Society and History* 37, no. 2 (1995): 368–98.

Wachowski, Lana, and Lilly Wachowski. *The Matrix*. Warner Brothers, 1999.

Weber, Max. *The Protestant Ethic and the Spirit of Capitalism*. New York: Scribner's, 1958.

Whorf, Benjamin Lee. *Language, Thought and Reality: Selected Writings of Benjamin Lee Whorf*. Edited by John B. Carroll. Cambridge, MA: MIT Press, 1956.

Wittfogel, Karl A. *Oriental Despotism: A Comparative Study of Total Power*. New Haven, CT: Yale University Press, 1957.

Yu, George T. *Asia's New World Order*. New York: New York University Press, 1997.

Žižek, Slavoj. *Looking Awry: An Introduction to Jacques Lacan through Popular Culture*. Cambridge, MA: MIT Press, 1992.

Žižek, Slavoj. *The Plague of Fantasies*. London: Verso, 1997.

Žižek, Slavoj. *The Sublime Object of Ideology*. London: Verso, 2008.

INDEX

hauntology (*continued*)
    literature and, 21–23, 36, 42–7; onto-
    logical turn and, 19, 25

immateriality: vs. materiality, 12–13, 153
IMF (International Monetary Fund), 75,
    79, 85

loan godmothers, 75, 96–100, 105, 166
Loevlie, Elizabeth, 21–22
lottery, 3, 66, 73, 75, 77, 80, 158–164

Mae Nak Shrine, 59–63
matter and the ontological turn, 18–19
Marx, Karl, 4, 6, 37
McLean, Stuart, 172n33
money, 6–7, 66
moral hazard, 82–83, 121–123
Morrison, Toni, 28

Nang Nak, 48–50, 57, 58
Negri, Antonio, 6, 67–72
numbers, 3–4, 40–43, 72, 83–88, 134–35,
    158–164

ontological turn, 15–19

prophecy: economics and, 83, 85; num-
    bers and, 83–8

realism, 22, 25–6, 42, 153; and anthro-
    pology and, 4–5, 22; seriousness and,
    16–17, 29 Freud and, 51–52; fiction and,
    7; economics and, 36, 83, 87, 119; eco-
    nomic irreality and, 86
metaphysics of presence, 22, 27–28
reality: as a medium, 56, 57
Ringu, 57

seriousness, 16–18. *See also* ontological
    turn
science fiction: social science and, 65, 67–72
Smith, Adam, 6–7
social constructionism, 4, 18–19
spectral metaphor, 1, 6. *See also* tropologi-
    cal spectralism
spectres of Marx, 20, 25–6, 31
spirit possession, 76–77, 145–148, 157

teak, 9–10
trees, 8–10, 13–14
tropological spectralism, 26. *See also*
    spectral metaphor

uncanny, 30, 46–47, 51–57

writing, 16–17, 25

Žižek, Slavoj, 6